FRANCE PROFILED

FRANCE
PROFILED

Essential facts on society, business and politics in France

Edited by Barry Turner

ST.MARTIN'S PRESS
NEW YORK

FRANCE PROFILED

St Martin's Press, Scholarly and Reference Division,
175 Fifth Avenue, New York, N.Y. 10010

First published in the United States of America in 1999

Printed in the United Kingdom

ISBN: 0–312–22723–x

Library of Congress Cataloging-in-Publication Data is available

Contents

Colour maps fall between pages 106 and 107

FRANCE

République Française

Capital: Paris

Area: 549,090 sq. km

Population estimate, 2000: 59·06m.

Head of State: Jacques Chirac

Head of Government: Lionel Jospin

TERRITORY AND POPULATION

France is bounded in the north by the English Channel *(La Manche)*, north-east by Belgium and Luxembourg, east by Germany, Switzerland and Italy, south by the Mediterranean (with Monaco as a coastal enclave), south-west by Spain and Andorra, and west by the Atlantic Ocean. The total area is 549,090 sq. km. Paris is the most populous agglomeration in Europe, with a population of over 9·3m. More than 14% of the population of Paris are foreign and 19% are foreign born.

Population (1990 census), 56·6m. Estimate (1996), 58·2m.

The UN gives a projected population for 2000 of 59·06m.; projection (2025), 61·2m. Density (1996), 106 persons per sq. km. In 1995 an estimated 74·7% of the population lived in urban areas.

The growth of the population has been as follows:

Census	Population	Census	Population	Census	Population
1801	27,349,003	1931	41,834,923	1968	49,778,540
1861	37,386,313	1946	40,506,639	1975	52,655,802
1901	38,961,945	1954	42,777,174	1982	54,334,871
1921	39,209,518	1962	46,519,997	1990	56,615,100

According to the 1990 census, there were 3·5m. people of foreign extraction in France (7·4% of the population). The largest groups of foreign residents (1992) were: Portuguese (649,714), Algerians (614,207) and Moroccans (572,652). 92,410 persons were naturalized in 1995 (126,337 in 1994).

Controls on illegal immigration were tightened in July 1991. Automatic right to citizenship for those born on French soil was restored in 1997 by the new left-wing coalition government. New immigration legislation, which was due to come into force in 1998, brought in harsher penalties for organized traffic in illegal immigrants and extended asylum laws to include people whose lives are at risk from non-state as well as state groups. It also extended nationality at the age of 18 to those born in France of non-French parents, provided they have lived a minimum of 5 years in France since the age of 11.

The areas, populations and chief towns of the 22 metropolitan regions at the 1990 census were as follows:

Regions	Area (sq. km)	Population	Chief town
Alsace	8,280	1,624,400	Strasbourg
Aquitaine	41,308	2,795,800	Bordeaux
Auvergne	26,013	1,321,200	Clermont-Ferrand
Basse-Normandie	17,589	1,391,300	Caen
Bourgogne (Burgundy)	31,582	1,609,700	Dijon
Bretagne (Brittany)	27,208	2,795,600	Rennes
Centre	39,151	2,371,000	Orléans
Champagne-Ardenne	25,606	1,347,900	Reims
Corse (Corsica)	8,680	250,400	Ajaccio
Franche-Comté	16,202	1,097,400	Besançon
Haute-Normandie	12,317	1,737,200	Rouen
Île-de-France	12,012	10,660,600	Paris
Languedoc-Roussillon	27,376	2,114,900	Montpellier
Limousin	16,942	722,800	Limoges
Lorraine	23,547	2,305,700	Nancy
Midi-Pyrénées	41,348	2,430,700	Toulouse
Nord-Pas-de-Calais	12,414	3,965,100	Lille
Pays de la Loire	32,082	3,059,200	Nantes
Picardie	19,399	1,810,700	Amiens
Poitou-Charentes	25,810	1,595,100	Poitiers
Provence-Alpes-Côte d'Azur	31,400	4,257,900	Marseilles
Rhône-Alpes	43,698	5,350,800	Lyons

ADMINISTRATIVE REGIONS

Alsace

Main Cities: Strasbourg, Mulhouse.

Départements: Bas-Rhin, Haut-Rhin, Territoire de Belfort.

Alsace is situated at the eastern edge of France and, along with Lorraine, has belonged to her neighbour, Germany on and off over the centuries. The influences in the region and the people, their dialect, architecture and cuisine, all have a distinctive Germanic feel. Alsace is famous for its wines (the history of Alsatian wines predates even the Romans), as well as beers and a particularly fierce Eau de Vie. Even though Mulhouse and Strasbourg are important industrial centres, the countryside of Alsace is largely unspoilt. Strasbourg is the capital city of Alsace and is situated on the banks of the Rhine, which has made it an important centre for commercial river traffic over the centuries. Nowadays the city is the seat of the European Parliament. Although small and compact, the city is important as an economic and administrative centre and is set to become a dynamic European centre with a high standard of living and good housing and facilities. Industries include mining, minerals, heavy engineering, automotive, textiles, brewing and wine production. Mulhouse is a centre for heavy industry whose rapid development is due primarily to its connections and proximity with Germany and its central position in Europe. Tourist attractions include the city of Strasbourg with its many museums and fine cathedral. The Routes des Vins offer the visitor the chance to travel around from town to town, enjoying the sights and tasting the various wines of the region. The Parc Naturel Régional des Ballons des Vosges is a national park set in 3,000 km of mountainous scenery. In winter there is skiing and in summer, hiking and cycling on hundreds of kilometres of specially constructed trails.

Aquitaine

Main City: Bordeaux (for more detailed information on Bordeaux, see page 87).

Départements: Dordogne, Gironde, Landes, Lot-et-Garonne, Pyrénées-Atlantiques.

Aquitaine is a large region of southwest France, probably best known by holidaymakers and wine experts. The Garonne, Lot and Dordogne valleys are very popular with holidaymakers and many foreigners have homes there. The region is primarily agricultural, including some of France's most famous vineyards. Despite the general decline in shipping traffic since the loss of the French colonies, Bordeaux has remained an important port for the import and export trade but the town is justly most famous for its wine production. Other industries in the area include aerospace, aeronautics, electronics, agri-foodstuffs and wood pulp. It is also a base for the manufacture of high technology equipment of various kinds.

Auvergne

Main city: Clermont-Ferrand.

Départements: Allier, Cantal, Haute-Loire, Puys de Dôme.

The Auvergne region contains some of the most remote regions of France although the arrival of the A71 Autoroute, which connects the area with Paris 300 km away, has meant the area is not nearly so isolated. The Massif Central, the third most mountainous area of France after the Alps and the Pyrenees, gives the region the breathtaking scenery of extinct volcanoes. Apart from the industrial towns (most notably Clermont-Ferrand and St. Etienne), the whole area has remained relatively unchanged – sparsely populated but with a rich architectural heritage of châteaux and churches in small provincial towns. Clermont-Ferrand is an important academic town and in addition to a wide range of light manufacturing industries, the major industrial giant and principal employer is the Michelin Tyre Company.

St. Etienne is a heavy industry and mining town. The region is also principally concerned with agricultural production – beef cattle and cheese production being the most important. There is a small amount or tourism, mostly centred on the various spa towns – Vichy being the best known.

Bourgogne (Burgundy)

Main City: Dijon.

Départements: Côte d'Or, Nievre, Saône-et-Loire, Yonne.

Burgundy runs from the small medieval town of Auxerre in the north almost to Lyon in the south. The countryside is not industrialized and the region owes its prosperity to the large quantity and superior quality of the wines produced throughout the area. Nuits St. Georges, Mersault, Chasagne-Montrachet, Mercurey and Pouilly-Fuissé are just some of the famous names to be found here. Burgundy was an independent kingdom for six hundred years and was at the height of its powers in the Middle Ages. At that time, many of the vineyards were run by monastic orders whose expertise in cultivation and distillation were the most highly developed in Europe. Although most of the area's traditional heavy industry has now declined, prominent industries still include iron and steel, engineering, glass, ceramics and motor manufacture. The cities of Mâcon and Bourg-en-Bresse are more industrialized than Dijon and throughout the region, tourism, based on the region's gastronomic and architectural heritage, is important. Although parts of Burgundy are remote and isolated, there is excellent access to Lyon and Paris by the A6 Autoroute that runs though the middle of the region.

Bretagne (Brittany)

Main Cities: Rennes, Brest and Nantes.

Départements: Côtes du Nord, Finistère, Ille-et-Vilaine, Morbihan.

The ancient Breton language is one of a group of languages that include Gaelic and Cornish and are believed to have been spoken by pre-Roman tribes of Britain and Gaul. The language is still spoken, albeit by a dwindling number of older inhabitants of the region. Other associations with Britain exist including trading links with Cornwall, Wales and Ireland that can be traced back hundreds of years. The rugged coastline and cliffs along with the unspoiled countryside attracts foreign (especially British) visitors each year. Tourism remains an important part of the region's economy even though, because of the uncertain weather, the season is limited to the summer months (May to October). Rennes is the capital of the region and is the academic and administrative centre, providing centres of research and development of many kinds. Companies that have made their headquarters in Rennes include printers, publishers, motor and automotive manufacturers and telecommunications organizations. The port of Brest has recently attracted large numbers of engineering and electronics industries. The region's agriculture produces fruit and vegetables and is France's most important area for pig production.

Champagne-Ardenne
Main City: Reims.
Départements: Ardennes, Aube, Haute-Marne, Marne.
The chalky soil of the rolling landscapes of the region impart special properties to the crops grown here, especially the grape that produces the most famous French wine of all, Champagne. The production of this sparkling white wine has dominated the life of this region since, in the 17th century, a blind monk accidentally discovered that stopping the bottles of fermenting wine with corks made them pop when drawn, whereupon he is said to have exclaimed 'je bois des etoiles' (I am drinking the stars). There is a new Autoroute under construction that will link Calais with Dijon and will greatly improve the communications of the region with the rest of France. The traditional

heavy engineering, steelworks, mining and textiles manufacturing of this region are slowly being replaced by the manufacture of electronics and agri-foodstuffs. Otherwise the region's prosperity depends on cereal crops and other agriculture and, of course, champagne.

Corse (Corsica)

Main cities: Ajaccio and Bastia.

Départements: Haute-Corse, Corse du Sud.

Corsica is an island in the Mediterranean Sea and is closer to the coast of Italy than to France, with a greater measure of autonomy than other regions of France and speaking its own unique mixture of Italian and French. Until 1768 Corsica was a much fought over territory when France bought the island from the then independent maritime kingdom of Genoa. Christopher Columbus and Napoleon were both born in Corsica and one of Napoleon's descendants, Prince Charles Napoleon, returned to live on the island in 1997. The island is only 180 km long and 80 km wide, sparsely populated, very mountainous (20 or so peaks rising as high as 2,000 metres) with tree covered slopes – the pine trees that grow there are highly prized as ship's masts. The island has virtually no industry, is sparsely populated and depends heavily on tourism (much of it domestic) for its prosperity. The island's railway was inaugurated in 1888 with 230 km of track, 12 bridges (including a 300 ft high viaduct built by Gustav Eiffel) and 38 tunnels. There is a university in Bastia (the island's commercial capital) and the spectacular land through the centre of the island is protected as a National Park.

Côte d'Azur

Main City: Nice.

Département: Alpes-Maritimes.

The Côte d'Azur is a large single-département region with most of the southern coastline of France along its southern border. The region's eastern border is with Italy and the interior reaches inland only about 50 km into the foothills of the Alps. The tiny country of Monaco, which is encompassed in the region's coastline, is an entirely independent principality. The region is the most fashionable in France and a favourite holiday destination for visitors from all over the world. The property prices and cost of living in the region are among the highest in France. The exclusive and elegant resorts that run along the coastline, almost one into the other, have famous names like Cannes, Nice, Antibes, Juan-les-Pins, St.-Jean-Cap-Ferrat and Menton. The climate is mild in winter and hot in summer, and during the last century it was fashionable to come to the area for the winter from more northern climes. Although the area's thriving tourist industry, together with its convention and exhibition industry, are the largest contributors to the region's economy, high-tech industries such as electronics, computing, telecommunications and marine industries are to be found here, especially in Sophia Antipolis near Nice which is rapidly becoming one of the most important high-tech centres in France. The town of Grasse is the centre of the world's perfume industry with a large number of factories devoted to its production.

Franche Comté

Main City: Besançon.
Départements: Doubs, Haute Saône, Jura.
This region shares its long border as well as many of the influences in the culture, architecture and gastronomy with Switzerland. French workers living in the area where the cost of living is relatively modest are allowed to work across the border in Switzerland where the wages are considerably higher by means of a special work permit (the F permit). A higher percentage of the population of this region works in industry than any other in France. Besançon, the regional capital, is the clock-making centre of France and is famed for precision engineering. Montbéliard-Sochaux is home to the Peugeot car company

and other principal industries include light and heavy engineering, light assembly, textiles, mining and minerals. Elsewhere in the region small amounts of cheese, woodwork and craft products are produced and although the region is relatively unknown to foreign visitors, the scenery and landscape of the Jura Mountains are popular with French tourists.

Languedoc-Roussillon

Main Cities: Montpelier, Narbonne, Béziers.
Départements: Aude, Gard, Hérault, Lozère, Pyrènèes-Orientales.
The French regional development agency DATAR has invested heavily in this region and the resultant new found economic dynamism is attracting large numbers of new residents, both foreign and domestic. Languedoc is bordered by the Pyrenees, the Spanish frontier, the Mediterranean and the River Rhône and extends back into the Massif Central. This gives the area a rich and varied range of scenery from mountains to coastal and river deltas, large cities and tiny medieval towns. Montpelier, capital city of Languedoc, is an important academic and research centre and industries include computers, electronics, medical equipment and research, and telecommunications. Perpignan and Nîmes are also concerned with high-technology based industries and, because of the amount of new inward investment, construction has become a major industry. Tourism adds a boost to the region's economy along the highly developed coastal strip while inland, wine production and agriculture (Mediterranean fruits and vegetables) are the main industries.

Limousin

Main City: Limoges.
Départements: Corrèze, Creuse, Haute-Vienne.
Limousin stands between the Mediterranean south of France and the industrial heartland of the north. The region is very scenic and

bordered on the east by the Auvergne and on the west by the Dordogne – both popular tourist areas. However, Limousin has the lowest property prices and cost of living in France, representing France at its most rural and tranquil. Although the principal industry is agriculture – mostly small-scale cattle farming – the region is world famous for the production of porcelain. The area also produces agri-foodstuffs and leather products and local cottage-style industries include metal work and glass. The regional authorities are trying to encourage new commercial opportunities and tourism.

Loire Valley (Centre)

Main Cities: Orléans, Chartres, Blois, Bourges, Tours.
Départements: Cher, Eure-et-Loir, Indre, Indre-et-Loire,
Loir-et-Cher, Loiret.

This region is so well connected to Paris by autoroutes (A10, A11 and A71 all serve the area) that it has become a popular commuter area for people working in Paris. Property prices and cost of living in the region are relatively high. The Châteaux of the Loire and the cathedral of Chartres, as well as the many other towns and villages of historic and architectural interest in the area, are world famous and millions of visitors are attracted to the region each year. Although food production, manufacturing and processing and agriculture form a strong part of the region's economy, tourism is the principal industry.

Loire-West (Pays de la Loire)

Main City: Nantes
Départements: Loire-Atlantique, Maine-et-Loire, Mayenne, Sarthe,
Vendée.

The industrial hub of the region is the Nantes-St. Lazare port complex, one of the largest in France. The region's main industries are electronics, engineering and garment and footwear manufacture. Other more traditional industries include food processing, maritime industries,

fishery, agriculture and wine production. New industries in development and research and telecommunications are being established.
Paris is only 2 hours away from Nantes, the regional capital, thanks to
the high-speed train (TGV) and the A11 Autoroute. The city also offers
good access to Brittany (of which it was once part) and the ports of
St. Malo on the Atlantic coastline and even Le Havre further north.
The romantically wild Atlantic coast is popular with tourists in the
summer while further inland the world-famous circuit of Le Mans
attracts motor-racing enthusiasts.

Lorraine (Lorraine-Vosges)

Main Cities: Nancy, Metz.
Départements: Meurthe-et-Moselle, Meuse, Moselle, Vosges.
Like her neighbour, Alsace, Lorraine has been part of Germany on
and off for centuries. Located in the extreme northeastern corner of
France, the region borders Germany on one side with Belgium and
Luxembourg on the others. Lorraine was also in the path of advancing
German troops during World War I and some of the towns bear the
names of famous battles – Verdun, Metz, etc. The area has good
access to other parts of France via the A26 and A4 autoroutes and is
easily accessible to visitors and commerce from the UK either by boat
via the port of Calais or by rail or car via the Channel Tunnel. The
economy of this region used to depend on old heavy industries like
iron, steel and coal production but these have mostly ceased to exist
and are being replaced by finance, banking, electronics and computers. Nancy is an important academic city as well as being an administrative, banking and commercial centre. Away from the cities, the
region is important for agriculture, food processing and textiles.

Nord-Pas-de-Calais

Main Cities: Lille (for more detailed information on Lille, see page 83),
Calais, Dunkerque.

Départements: Nord de Calais, Pas de Calais.

This region is not only one of the smallest in France, but one of the most densely populated. The urban sprawl, made up of several large cities (including Lille, Roubaix, Tourcoing and Arras) spreads across the border into Belgium. Lille is only 90 km from Brussels and they are soon to be linked by a new Autoroute, the A8. The region is experiencing a boom in development owing to recent government incentives to attract inward investment, which should help to solve the current unemployment problem. The traditional industries of mining and steel production are gradually being replaced by electronics, transport, distribution services and energy related industries. Over 400 international companies, some of them British (including Whessoe, BP, Courtaulds, K.P. Foods and P&O) have moved to the area, taking advantage of the increased opportunities offered by the Channel Tunnel and the TGV high speed rail links to Paris, Lille, Brussels, etc. Lille is one of France's largest cities, particularly noted for its modern and efficient public transport system and offers good housing and excellent facilities to the people who work in the surrounding towns of the industrial conurbation. Although the whole region is largely industrialized, there are pockets of unspoilt countryside and picturesque towns.

Normandie (Normandy)

Main Cities: Rouen, Le Havre, Dieppe, Cherbourg.

Départements: Calvados, Eure, Manche, Orne, Seine-Maritime.

Normandy has close associations with the UK, not only physically via the ports of Dieppe, Le Havre and Cherbourg, but also historically. William the Conqueror set off from Normandy to invade Britain in 1066, and several centuries later the Allies landed on the Normandy beaches on D-Day in 1944 at the start of the end of World War II. The coastal resorts of Le Touquet and Deauville have been favourite grand watering holes of the British since the 19th century. Normandy

is one of the few regions of France that does not produce wine but it is famous for the excellence of its rich food. The region produces apples, from which are made cider and a form of very strong apple-brandy, Calvados. Heavy industry is concentrated in the Seine valley and around the ports of Rouen and Le Havre. Industries include heavy engineering, metal industries, motor manufacture, chemicals, petrochemicals, pharmaceuticals and plastics. New industry is being introduced into the region including electronics and telecommunications. Apart from this industrial area, Normandy is a largely agricultural and rural region producing dairy products, livestock and fruit.
Tourism is important and with the ease of access to Paris, Normandy has become a popular region for commuters and weekenders.

Paris and Ile de France

Main City: Paris (for more detailed information on Paris see page 65).
Départements: Paris, Region Parisienne, Seine-et-Marne.
Paris is the capital city of France. It is the seat of government, houses the headquarters of many international bodies (including UNESCO and the OECD), has the largest population of any region in France and is surrounded by the biggest concentration of industrial and commercial development in France. Some heavy industry still exists in the city itself (mostly motor manufacture) but the surrounding outer suburbs are commercial and business centres in their own right and most of the industry is located there. As befits a capital city, Paris is a Mecca for millions of tourists. Although the city has a high cost of
living and property prices are higher here than anywhere else in France, the city is also noted for its cheap and very efficient public transport system. This includes the Métro (underground) and the RER suburban trains system which bring many of the outlying areas into the range of commuters.

Somewhat surprisingly, the hinterland around Paris is extremely fertile and is important for agriculture.

Picardie (Picardy)

Main Cities: Amiens, Beauvais, Compiègne, Chantilly.

Départements: Aisne, Oise, Somme.

Picardy is historically associated with battlefields from both world wars and the armistice that ended the First World War in the Forest of Compiègne. The large flat fields provide the region with cereals and industrial crops. Some iron and steel-based heavy industry still exists in the region while other newer industries include chemicals, tyre manufacture, engineering and textiles. There have been developments in the production of agri-foodstuffs and tourism is on the increase. Property prices and cost of living are among the lowest in France.

Poitou and Charentes

Main City: Poitiers.

Départements: Charente, Charente-Maritime, Deux-Sèvres, Vienne.

Poitiers was once the capital of Aquitaine and marks the linguistic boundary between the langue d'oie of northern France and the langue d'oc of the southern provinces. Today, the region consists of two sub-regions formed into one administrative region. La Rochelle and Roquefort on the Atlantic coast are resort towns with a big tourist trade while Poitiers is the commercial centre for local businesses. There is little industry – agriculture (mainly beef cattle) and fisheries provide most of the region's jobs. The region produces France's finest brandy in the area around the town of Cognac.

Provence

Main Cities: Marseilles (for more detailed information on Marseilles, see page 80), Toulon, Aix-en-Provence, Avignon.

Départements: Alpes-de-Haute-Provence, Bouches-du-Rhône, Hautes-Alpes, Var, Vaucluse.

The terrain of Provence is partly mountainous, partly hilly and partly flat. It lies along the south coast next to the Côte d'Azur and is famous for its tourist resorts and historic towns. Provence also has a great deal of industry, mostly around the cities of Marseilles and Toulon – both major ports. Marseilles is also a major international city, densely populated with an industrial hinterland spreading both to the east and west of the city. The port of Marseilles is the gateway from France to North Africa and Corsica and this creates an extremely cosmopolitan atmosphere. Marseilles is traditionally a heavy industry area, most of which still exists although on a reduced scale. Industries include chemicals, oil, textiles, pharmaceuticals, heavy engineering, iron, steel and shipyards. Marseilles and Toulon are also major distribution centres involved in maritime and shipping services and research. New growth industries in Marseilles include electronics, computing, aerospace and light high-technology manufacturing. The region's countryside is largely agricultural, growing Mediterranean produce but the region has attracted a very large number of foreign holiday-makers, many of whom have bought property, and the prices are high, as is the cost of living.

Midi-Pyrénées
Main City: Toulouse (for more detailed information on Toulouse, see page 92.)
Départements: Ariège, Aveyron, Gers, Haute-Garonne, Hautes-Pyrénées, Lot, Tarn, Tarn-et-Garonne.
The Midi-Pyrénées is one of the largest in France and is bordered on the northeast by Aquitaine and on the southeast by Languedoc-Rousillon. Toulouse is something of an economic boomtown with nearly all its industries in the growth area of high technology. Industries include aeronautics, aerospace, aviation, electronics, data processing, computers and robotics. Toulouse is also an important academic and research centre with a fine old university and has many

government offices as well as historic buildings and several art museums of note. The Pyrenees part of the region is mainly agricultural producing traditional crops and wine. The region comprises many different types of scenery, from the mountains of the Pyrenees to the Tarn valley with its dramatic gorges and the high plateaux of Aveyron. The whole region attracts considerable numbers of tourists each year and in particular the region of Gascony (Gascogne) is popular with British visitors. The hundred or so walled towns in the area were built by the English 600 years ago when the area came under the English crown. The region is linked by autoroutes and Paris is only approximately five hours away with Lyon, Bordeaux, Spain and the south coast all within relatively easy reach. Wages in the region are high but so are property prices and the cost of living.

Rhône (The Rhône Valley)

Main City: Lyon (for more detailed information about Lyon see page 74).

Départements: Ain, Ardèche, Drôme, Loire, Rhône.

With the Seine, the Rhône is one of France's two main rivers and this region takes in the broad valley and plain of the river Rhône between the Alps and the Massif Central. The area is a focal point for industrial activity and this has made the region one of the fastest expanding areas in France. Lyon is France's second city as far as commerce is concerned and the city's conurbation is France's second largest manufacturing and services area. The newer industries in the area include computing, electronics and communications, although older more traditional industries such as textiles, chemicals, petrochemicals and motor manufacture still exist. Despite the heavy concentration of industry, Lyon is also known for its agriculture plus some wine growing. The city is said to be the gastronomic capital of France, providing the world with many of its finest chefs. Lyon is within easy reach by either TGV or Autoroute of Switzerland, Paris and the south of France.

Property prices and cost of living are both high as the area attracts large numbers of people in search of employment.

Savoie & Dauphiny

Main City: Grenoble.

Départements: Isère, Haute-Savoie, Savoie.

The French administration regards Savoy and Dauphiny as one administrative entity although they are historically two separate regions. The region lies in the French Alps, with nearly all of France's ski resorts within its borders, The area shares extensive borders with Switzerland and Italy, sharing cultural influences with both countries. Savoy with Dauphiny is perhaps the most scenic region of France with breathtaking mountainous scenery and unspoiled countryside. The capital city of Grenoble is a rapidly growing French 'Techno-city' with high-tech industries that include electronics, computing and telecommunications. The area is also the centre of the French nuclear industry and Grenoble, which boasts a famous university, is an important academic, scientific research centre. Other more traditional industries include engineering, mining and minerals, and textiles. Although there is a fair amount of tourism in the summer, in winter the whole region is invaded by hundreds of thousands of tourists for the ski season.

Populations of the principal conurbations (in descending order of size) and towns at the 1990 census:

	Conurbation	Town		Conurbation	Town
Paris	9,318,82[1]	2,152,423	Bordeaux	696,364	210,336
Lyons	1,262,223[2]	415,487	Toulouse	650,336	358,688
Marseilles-Aix-			Nice	516,740	342,439
en-Provence	1,230,936[3]	800,550	Nantes	496,078	244,995
Lille	959,234[4]	172,142	Toulon	437,553	167,619

Grenoble	404,733	150,758	Thionville	132,413	40,835
Strasbourg	388,483	252,338	Saint-Nazaire	131,511	64,812
Rouen	380,161	102,723	Annecy	126,729	51,143
Valenciennes	338,392	39,276	Troyes	122,763	59,271
Cannes	335,647	68,676	Besançon	122,623	113,828
Nancy	329,447	99,351	Montbéliard	117,510	30,639
Lens	323,174	35,278	Lorient	115,488	59,437
Saint-Étienne	313,338	197,536	Hagondange-Briey	112,061	9,091
Tours	282,152	129,509	Valence	107,965	63,437
Béthune	261,535	25,261	Melun	107,705	36,489
Clermont-Ferrand	254,416	136,181	Poitiers	107,625	78,894
Le Havre	253,627	195,854	Chambéry	103,283	54,120
Montpellier	248,303	207,996	Angoulême	102,908	46,194
Rennes	245,065	199,396	Maubeuge	102,772	35,225
Orléans	243,153	105,111	Calais	101,768	75,309
Dijon	230,451	146,703	La Rochelle	100,264	71,094
Mulhouse	223,856	108,357	Forbach	98,758	27,357
Angers	208,282	141,404	Creil	97,119	32,501
Reims	206,437	180,620	Bourges	94,731	75,609
Brest	201,480	147,956	Cherbourg	92,045	28,773
Douai	199,562	44,195	Boulogne-sur-Mer	91,249	44,244
Metz	193,117	119,594	Chartres	85,933	41,850
Caen	191,490	112,846	Saint-Brieuc	83,861	47,370
Dunkerque	190,879	70,331	Colmar	83,816	63,498
Le Mans	189,107	145,502	Saint-Chamond	81,795	39,262
Mantes-la-Jolie	189,103	45,254	Tarbes	80,680	50,228
Avignon	181,136	86,939	Arras	79,607	42,715
Limoges	170,065	133,464	Belfort	78,215	50,125
Bayonne	164,378	41,846	Chalon-sur-Saône	77,764	54,575
Perpignan	157,873	105,983	Roanne	77,160	42,848
Amiens	156,120	131,872	Alès	76,856	–
Pau	144,674	82,157	Béziers	76,304	70,996
Nîmes	138,527	128,471			

[1] Including Boulogne-Billancourt (101,743), Montreuil (94,754), Argenteuil (93,096), Versailles (87,789), Saint-Denis (89,988), Nanterre (84,565), Vitry-sur-Seine (82,400), Aulnay-sous-Bois (82,314), Créteil (82,088).

[2] Including Villeurbanne (116,872), Vénissieux (60,644).

[3] Including Aix-en-Provence (123,842).

[4] Including Roubaix (97,746), Tourcoing (93,765).

KEY HISTORICAL EVENTS

Much of our knowledge of pre-historic times comes from the abundant remains to be found all over France. Traces of early settlements with wall decorations are to be found in the caves of the Dordogne, the Pyrenees and the Ardeche; the most famous of these are the caves at Lascaux, which were discovered by schoolchildren in 1940. By the beginning of the 8th century BC, Celtic tribes from central Europe were established in the Rhône valley of Gaul (now France) while the Greeks were building cities such as Marseilles (Massilia) along the southern coast. But it was not until the 2nd century BC that the Celts began to give way to Germanic and Roman influences. The Romans had passed through the Alps into southern France in 121 BC, and Gaul was conquered by Julius Caesar in 52 BC when the whole of France (roughly as we know it today) became part of the Roman Empire. It not only profited from 'Pax Romana' and the protection it brought to the country's trade routes but benefited from Roman culture, infrastructure, speech and government. During the reign of Augustus at the end of the 1st century, Roman rule in Gaul was consolidated and expanded but the Empire was declining. The Moors were constantly attacking the southern ports and, to the north, barbarians mounted a succession of invasions. Many of these invaders were assimilated into the Gallo-Roman Empire but after the repulse of Attila and his Huns in 451, the Salian Franks emerged as the strongest of the barbarian tribes under their leader Merovius. He gave his name to the dynasty (Merovingians) that was to rule France until the beginning of the 8th century.

After Christianity spread from the south, Clovis, grandson of Merovius, was baptised in Reims in 496 and made Paris his capital. On his death the kingdom was divided between his three sons and although the Merovingians remained in power for a further two centuries, their rule was weakened by internecine warfare. In 751 the last of the Merovingians was deposed and the Carolingian dynasty was founded. Having extended his empire over Germany and Italy, Charlemagne was crowned Emperor of the West in 800. He moved his seat of government to Aix-la-Chapelle where he presided over a remarkable revival of learning and education. However, the Empire was divided up into territories on Charlemagne's death and in 843, the Treaty of Verdun divided the Carolingian Empire between his grandsons, the sons of Louis I (the Pious). Charles le Chauve received the western territories, an area roughly corresponding to modern day France. But France was under attack from all sides. By 912 Vikings had settled in Rouen having laid siege to Paris. Further threats came from Muslim Saracens in the south and Hungarian Magyars in the east. The Carolingians struggled to keep their power for another hundred years but they were years of unrest and disunity for France.

In 987 Hugh Capet, Duke of France, ousted Charles of Lorraine and had himself elected King. To consolidate his family's rule his son was crowned before he came into his inheritance. To control the disunited country, power was centralized on Paris. In 910 the great Benedictine Abbey of Cluny was founded. During the next hundred years, several more Abbeys were built in a wave of religious fervour. Of less credit to the Church were the early crusades to the Holy Land, the expulsion of the Jews by Philippe Auguste in 1182 and the bloody

Albigensian crusade against the heretical Cathars of Languedoc in 1209. In 1214 Philippe Auguste won back the provinces of Normandy and Anjou from John of England although it was not until 1259 that Henry III formally surrendered Normandy after his defeat at Saintes by Louis IX.

Between 1150 and 1300, France underwent a period of expansion and building. Most of the major cathedrals of France were either erected or reconstructed and many new towns were founded (notably the 'bastides' or fortified towns of southwest France with their still recognizable grid pattern streets) while most of the older cities grew in size and prosperity.

In 1309 Pope Clement V was expelled from Rome and set up his papal court at Avignon where the popes remained until 1377 (when two anti-popes took their place, remaining there until driven out in 1403). The last Capetian king, Charles IV, died in 1328 (leaving only daughters) and the Capetian dynasty gave way to the House of Valois. However, King Edward III of England disputed the claim of Philippe de Valois. This marked the start of the Hundred Years War between the Plantaganets and the Capetians over who should rule France. With his son, the Black Prince, Edward III invaded France where a series of victories led to the Treaty of Brétigny in 1360, which ceded Aquitaine to England. Edward renounced all claims to the French throne but the warfare continued until bit by bit the French, under Charles V, won back most of their lost territories. Another invasion was led, in 1415, by Henry V of England who, with the backing of the Burgundians, defeated the French at Agincourt. He married the daughter of Charles IV and obtained the right of succession to the French throne. After his death and that of Charles IV only seven weeks later, the new king enlisted the help of Jeanne d'Arc (Joan of Arc), who conducted a series of brilliant campaigns against the English. Although she was eventually captured, tried as a heretic by a court of Burgundian Ecclesiastics and burnt at the stake in Rouen in 1431, the

French successes continued and eventually the English were driven from all their French possessions except Calais.

The reign of Louis XI saw a change from a medieval social system to a more modern state. Provincial governments were set up in major cities and nobles wielding independent power were crushed. At the same time, the invention of the printing press in Germany by Johannes Gutenberg in 1450 helped the spread of new thinking, much of it inspired by the Italian Renaissance. It was at this time that the great châteaux of the Loire valley were created as royal residences.

François I acceded to the throne of France in 1515. His reign saw the foundation of modern French law and the creation of a new sense of nationalism, replacing the earlier provincialism. In 1541 Calvin published his *Institutes of the Christian Religion*, generally regarded as the first great classic of French literature. In 1562 France was caught between the two branches of Christianity. A civil war (the Wars of Religion) raged between the protestant Huguenots (including the Bourbons) and the Catholic League supported by Spain. Hopes for peace, founded on the Treaty of St. Germain in 1570, were set back two years later by the St. Bartholomew's massacre which killed 20,000 Huguenots. In 1583 the war finally came to an end when Bourbon, Henry of Navarre, the Huguenot leader, converted to Catholicism and managed to unite France. He did not abandon his protestant roots and the Edict of Nantes in 1598 guaranteed the political and religious rights of Protestants.

After Henry's assassination in 1610, the young Louis XIII took the throne but, as he was too young to rule, his mother, Marie de Médicis, acted as Regent. In 1624, Cardinal Richelieu took the reins of government and set about establishing absolute royal power in France, with the suppression of any Protestant influences in politics. He went on to turn his attention to the House of Hapsburg, who under the Emperor Charles V had been nibbling at the eastern frontiers of France.

Richelieu formed an alliance with Gustavus Adolphus of Sweden to wage the Thirty Years' War on Charles V. As well as his many military and political achievements, Richelieu founded the Académie Française in 1635. When Richelieu died in 1642, his position was taken by Cardinal Mazarin, who continued with his predecessor's policies. After 20 years of disastrous civil war (known as the Fronde), Mazarin died and Louis XIV, who had succeeded as a minor in 1643, was able to govern alone. Operating under the tenet "L'Etat c'est moi", Louis XIV selected his ministers from among the haute bourgeoisie, reducing the nobility to the role of ineffectual courtiers. He then embarked on a series of military campaigns devoted primarily to self-aggrandizement. Five days after his succession (at the age of five years), the French defeated the Spanish, ending the Thirty Years' War and Spain's dominance of Europe's affairs. France's claim to Alsace (apart from Strasbourg and Mulhouse) was upheld. The rapid campaign of 1667–68 procured several towns in Flanders while the Dutch War of 1672–78 ended in the Peace of Nijmegen and the absorption into France of the Franche-Comte. Less successful were the campaigns against the League of Augsburg (or the Grand Alliance) in 1686–97 and the War of the Spanish Succession (1701–13) in which French forces suffered repeatedly at the hands of the Duke of Marlborough and Prince Eugene. England withdrew from the war in 1712 after the French victory at Denain. Meanwhile, the king revoked the Edict of Nantes and once again imposed Catholicism on France. Protestant churches were destroyed and religious minorities were persecuted.

The court of Louis XIV moved to Versailles in 1672, where the king converted a small hunting lodge into a 14,000-room palace fit for the 'Roi Soleil'. Writers, playwrights, philosophers and composers gathered there to make Louis XIV's court a glittering monument to him.

Louis XV succeeded Louis XIV in 1715 (when he was also only 5 years old) with the Duke of Orleans as his regent. His reign was remarkable for, on the one hand, frivolity, indecision and corruption and, on the other, a flowering of French culture with the likes of Voltaire, Rousseau, Montesquieu and Marivaux frequenting the fashionable salons of Paris. Many of the contemporary philosophers vehemently attacked the establishment and the clergy, undoubtedly sowing the seeds of revolution. Louis XV married Maria, the daughter of the deposed King of Poland, and drew France into the War of the Polish Succession. Further costly military disasters followed including the Seven Years' War in which France allied herself with Austria and saw the loss of her colonies in India, North America and the West Indies.

When Louis XVI succeeded to the throne in 1774, the French people were unhappy with his predecessor's extravagance, corruption and lack of military success. He was too weak to cope with the growing financial crises caused by prolonged military failure and exacerbated by several years of bad harvests. In 1787–88 there were grain riots all over France but especially in Paris, Lyons, Nantes and Grenoble. These crises inspired reforms, but they were rejected by the privileged classes (les privilégiés), the upper ranks of the clergy (the First Estate) and the majority of the nobility (the Second Estate), who feared a reduction in their powers and tax-levying privileges. Meanwhile Louis XVI supported the American colonies in their struggle for independence from England, a policy that was financially disastrous and also did much to disseminate revolutionary and democratic ideals at home.

The French Revolution erupted in 1789 when the Third Estate (the non-privéligiés) assumed power as the National Assembly (replacing the Estates General) and overthrew the government. Riots broke out all over France, culminating in the storming of the Bastille in Paris on 14 July. In 1791 the King and his unpopular Austrian consort, Marie-Antoinette, together with their children, were arrested trying to leave France; he was brought back to Paris where he was suspended from office. A new legislative assembly was formed and although the moderate 'Girondins' held power at the start, the more extreme followers of Danton, Robespierre and Marat – the Jacobins – seized power and in 1792 declared a Republic.

On 21 Jan. 1793 Louis XVI was guillotined in the Place de la Révolution. After his death a reign of terror followed in which thousands of people were guillotined. Marat was assassinated in July 1793, Danton was guillotined in 1794 and later that year, Robespierre, chief architect of the Reign of Terror, himself was beheaded. Despite the efforts of the royalists to re-establish a monarchy, the Directory of Five was appointed to run the country. One of these five, Barras, had been responsible for the promotion of a young Corsican, Napoleon Bonaparte, to the rank of General. During the next four years, Napoleon commanded the French troops in a series of successful campaigns against the Austrians and the British. On his return to Paris, he found the Directory in disarray and on 9 Nov. 1799, with the help of the army, Napoleon overthrew the government and had himself declared First Consul. In Nov. 1804 he asked Pope Pius VII to come to Paris and crown him Emperor of the first French Empire in Notre Dame de Paris. The Pope reluctantly agreed. At the moment of coronation, Napoleon took the crown from the Pope and placed it on his own head and then turned and crowned his wife, the Empress Josephine.

Napoleon immediately faced a hostile coalition of England, Austria and Russia. He had planned to invade England but, in 1805, after abandoning the idea, he shattered Austria and Russia at Austerlitz and imposed the humiliating Peace of Pressburg. The British naval victory at the Battle of Trafalgar earlier in the same year had given Britain control of the seas. Napoleon's best troops were bogged down supporting his brother Joseph in the Peninsula War in Spain where they met with repeated defeats at the hands of allied troops under the command of the Duke of Wellington. Napoleon marched on Russia in

1812 and although he was victorious at Borodino, his 'Grande Armée' was virtually annihilated crossing the Beresina. During the winter of 1812 he was forced into the infamous 'retreat from Moscow'. The Prussian army retaliated at Leipzig, entered France and forced the surrender of Paris in March 1814. Napoleon abdicated at Fontainbleau on 20 April 1814 and retired to Elba. Later that year King Louis XVIII returned from England where he had been exiled to restore the Bourbons, officially at least, to the throne. Napoleon returned from Elba and made a desperate attempt to regain absolute power. He made his way north towards Paris, gathering support along the way. But his defeat in 1815 at Waterloo by the Allies, led by the Duke of Wellington, marked the end of his 'Hundred Days' reign. He was exiled to the island of St. Helena where he died in 1821.

When Charles X succeeded Louis XVIII in 1824, he introduced his reactionary Ordinances de St. Cloud to suppress the liberty of the press and reduce the electorate to the landed classes. This provoked a revolution that, in July 1830, lost him his throne. Louis Phillipe, son of the Duke of Orléans, succeeded as constitutional monarch. France had a few large cities but was still largely a rural country. The neglect of the urban population helped to spread social-ist ideas. The 'Citizen King' attempted to defend himself from the people by surrounding Paris with a ring of fortifications but in 1848 the 'July Monarchy' was overthrown and, in the elections that followed (in which the electorate abruptly leapt from 250,000 to 9,000,000), Louis Napoleon, nephew of Bonaparte, was elected Prince/President thus inaugurating the 'Second Empire'. Emperor Napoleon III took the rather misleading title of "L'Empire, c'est la Paix" but instantly involved France in a succession of wars, first in the Crimea and then in an attempt to free Italy from Austrian oppression. In 1870 Louis Napoleon declared war on Prussia. Early defeats led to his capture. He was then deposed in 1870 and died in exile in Chislehurst (in England) in 1873.

In 1870 the Third Republic was proclaimed. But German troops were advancing on Paris and after a four-month siege and much suffering and starvation, Paris capitulated in Jan. 1871. By Sept. 1873 the occupying troops had gone and France was left to pick up the pieces. Alsace and Lorraine had been lost and French politics, embittered by the reprehensible 'Dreyfus' Affair (1894–1906) in which forged evidence resulted in the Jewish General Staff Captain being imprisoned for spying, went from crisis to crisis. An entente cordiale was established between France and England in 1904, putting a stop to colonial rivalry and paving the way for future co-operation. In 1905 the Church was separated from the State, an essential measure to counteract the influence the church and religious orders had on French education.

With Europe split into two tripartite factions – the triple entente (England, France and Russia) and the triple alliance (Germany, Italy and Hungary) – the stability of the continent was delicately balanced. A crisis in the Balkans (and the assassination of the Austrian arch-duke Ferdinand in Sarajevo) plunged France and her allies into war with Germany. A European war broke out on 3 Aug. 1914 and although Paris was saved from occupation, ten departments were overrun and four long years of trench warfare with appalling loss of life on both sides followed. The tide began to turn against Germany in 1916 with the Battle of the Somme, the French stand at Verdun and the arrival of the Americans in 1917. But the Armistice was not signed until 11 Nov. 1918. The provinces lost at the Treaty of Versailles in 1871 were restored to France but Clemenceau, the French Prime Minister, wanted more. The reparations demanded from Germany caused deep resentment and helped sow the seeds for World War II. By the end of the war France had lost a total of 1,300,000 men, apart from those maimed and wounded, and nothing could compensate her for this staggering loss of manpower.

Despite this, France slowly regained her strength although the political scene remained unstable. When the world was rocked by economic disruption, the demoralized German people turned to Adolf Hitler and his Nazi party to solve their economic and social problems. Hitler's expansionist policies once more threw Europe into conflict when he invaded Czechoslovakia and Poland. German troops advanced rapidly across northern Europe taking Holland and Belgium before crossing the frontier into France.

The main thrust of France's efforts to rebuild her defences after World War I had been concentrated on the 'Maginot Line' – a supposedly impregnable barrier running along the German frontier, but which was sidestepped by the advancing German forces in 1939. Demoralized French Troops, in no state to resist the German advance, were forced to retreat towards Dunkirk in northern France where the previously routed British Expeditionary Force managed to re-cross the Channel. The French government capitulated and a pro-German government presided over by Marshal Pétain (a hero of the Battle of Verdun in World War I) was established at Vichy. A truce was signed with Germany whereby the northern third of the country was occupied by the Germans while the southern portion was put under the control of the collaborationist government at Vichy. General Charles de Gaulle established the Forces Françaises Libres (Free French Forces) and declared the Comité National Français to be the true French government-in-exile with its headquarters first in London and then in Algiers. Meanwhile in France the Resistance continued to harass the German Army of occupation and gave secret aid to the Allies. De Gaulle returned at the head of the allied armies in Aug. 1944, liberated Paris and, with the Allies, signed an armistice with Germany in March 1945.

In Oct. 1946 the Fourth Republic, institutionally similar to the Third Republic, was established, but during prolonged wrangling over the form of the new constitution General de Gaulle retired. Women now had the vote and proportional representation was adopted. Slowly, despite frequent changes of government, defeat in Indo-China and a revolt in Algiers, France returned to economic prosperity. In 1957 a European 'common market' was established in which France, West Germany, Italy and the Benelux countries were founder members. In 1958 de Gaulle prepared a new constitution and was persuaded to return first as Prime Minster and then, by universal suffrage, as the first President of the newly declared Fifth Republic. In 1962, Algeria gained independence and in 1965 de Gaulle was returned to power, albeit with a reduced majority. De Gaulle was largely responsible for the substance of the Fifth Republic. Under the current constitution, the President of the Republic holds considerable power – he appoints the Prime Minster and the Council of Ministers and can, in extremis, dissolve the National Assembly (France's parliament).

After the end of World War II, the North Atlantic Treaty Organization (NATO) was set up to consolidate the Western defence. France was initially a member but de Gaulle became increasingly uncomfortable with NATO's policy of military integration and in 1966 he announced the withdrawal of French forces from the NATO consolidated command and ordered all NATO troops not under French command off French soil. NATO headquarters, which had been in Paris, moved to Brussels and France developed her own nuclear capability independent of NATO.

De Gaulle continued to preside over a period of relative stability and economic growth but serious student riots in Paris in 1968 precipitated overdue reforms. The students, who demanded reforms to the authoritarian system of education, were joined by workers who wanted more pay and better conditions. The National Assembly was dissolved and although the Gaullists were returned to power in the new election, de Gaulle's referendum proposing further decentralization was defeated and in 1969 he resigned. He died in 1970 at the age of 80.

Georges Pompidou, who had been de Gaulle's Prime Minister, succeeded him. Pompidou attempted to consolidate de Gaulle's legacy by concentrating on economic reform but he died in office in 1974. His successor, Giscard d'Estaing, was a brilliant intellectual whose determination to continue with these right-wing Gaullist policies precipitated a swing to the left. In 1981 François Mitterrand, a socialist, was elected to the Presidency. Within a couple of weeks of his election, Mitterrand had raised the minimum wage and instituted a compulsory fifth week of statutory holiday. He continued with other typically socialist legislation until a deep recession in 1983 forced him to take a series of unpopular deflationary measures. The elections of 1986 saw the emergence of a new ultra right-wing ultra nationalist racist party, the 'Front National' (FN) headed by Jean Marie Le Pen. The FN gained 10% of the vote. The socialists lost the elections when the Gaullist, Jacques Chirac, then Mayor of Paris, became Prime Minister. In 1988 Mitterrand was re-elected President with Edith Cresson as France's first woman Prime Minister. She resigned in 1992 and was succeeded by Pierre Bérégovoy, who was caught up in allegations of corruption. The socialists were defeated in the 1993 elections when Edouard Balladur of the centre-right RPR (Rassemblement pour la République) became Prime Minster. When the ailing Mitterrand's term of office expired in 1995, Jacques Chirac was elected President with Alain Juppé as Prime Minster. Mitterrand died in 1996. When the socialists returned to power in June 1997, Juppé resigned. Lionel Jospin now serves as a leftist Prime Minster, sharing power with the rightist President, Jacques Chirac.

Charles de Gaulle (1890–1970)

Charles André Joseph Marie de Gaulle was a soldier, statesman and founder of the Fifth Republic.

As a child, de Gaulle was fascinated by military tactics and battles. He was trained at the Academy of Saint-Cyr. In 1913 he joined an infantry regiment as Second Lieutenant. De Gaulle proved to be an exceptionally brave and talented soldier. During World War I, he fought at Verdun, was wounded three times, imprisoned for nearly three years and was three times mentioned in dispatches. After the war, de Gaulle's military career saw him as a military teacher and as a member of the Supreme War Council. He served with troops in the Rhineland and understood just how devastating the German military could be against inadequate French defences.

At the outbreak of World War II, de Gaulle was a Brigadier General serving in the 4th Armoured Division. After the French defeat, he fled to England from whence he launched his political career. On 2 Aug. 1940, a Vichy military court tried him and sentenced him to death, he was stripped of his military rank and all his property was confiscated.

Fiercely patriotic, de Gaulle set about establishing himself as a worthy leader of the French people. He advocated continued resistance against the German invaders as leader of the Françaises Libres (Free French). Yet his early political career in London was not auspicious. British politicians thought that he was obstinate and often fractious. In 1943, de Gaulle moved his headquarters to Algiers and became president of the French Committee of National Liberation.

After the end of World War II and subsequent struggle to rebuild a war-ravaged France, de Gaulle opposed the Fourth Republic believing that its policies and constitution would lead to much of the confusion and inadequacy of the Third Republic. In 1947, he formed the Rassemblement du peuple Français (Rally of the French People) which soon developed into a political party. In 1953, increasingly disillusioned by the party, de Gaulle severed his ties with the Rally of the French People and retired to his home in Colombey-les-Deux-Églises.

When, in 1958, insurrection broke out in Algiers, de Gaulle was recalled to power and was invested as Prime Minister. On 21 Dec. 1958 Charles de Gaulle was elected first President of the Fifth Republic, appointing Michel Debré as his Prime Minister. The Fifth Republic began on 8 Jan. 1959 when de Gaulle assumed his presidential functions and after he had established his intention and right to overhaul the constitution; this he did quickly.

On 8 March 1962, de Gaulle disenchanted his right-wing supporters by granting Algeria its independence.

De Gaulle's two terms as President were characterized by continuing friction with his parliament. In 1969, he resigned as President and retired to Colombey-les-Deux-Églises to continue writing his memoirs, having concluded 'that politics are too serious a matter to be left to the politicians'. He died of a heart attack in 1970.

CHRONOLOGY

Ancient Times
BC

5000   Megalithic culture flourishes.

8th century

Celtic tribes from central Europe build fortified settlements in Gaul.

6th century

Greek traders found cities in the south, including Marseilles.

2nd century

Celtic culture gives way to Germanic and Roman influences.

58–52   Julius Caesar's Gallic Wars.

AD

1st century

Roman rule is consolidated. Under Augustus, Gaul benefits from 'Pax Romana', Roman culture, speech, government and trade routes.

5th century

Foundation of early Christian monasteries.

The Merovingians

451   Defeat of Attila the Hun by Merovius, King of the Salian Franks.

476   Fall of the Roman Empire in the west. Gaul occupied by barbarian hordes.

496   King Clovis baptised in Reims.

6th century

Settlers from Britain arrive in Brittany.

The Carolingians

751   Pepin is elected king and sends the last of the Merovingians to a monastery.

800   Charlemagne is crowned Emperor of the West in Rome.

843   Treaty of Verdun divides the Empire between Charlemagne's grandsons. Charles the Bald receives the Western territory (roughly the France of today).

10th century

910   The foundation of the Abbey of Cluny heralds a wave of monastic fervour and building.

The Capetians

987   Hugh Capet, Duke of 'France' is elected king. He crowns his son in his own lifetime to secure succession.

11th century

1066   William Duke of Normandy successfully invades Britain and is crowned king.

1095   The First Crusade to the Holy Land.

12th century

1137   Louis VII marries Eleanor of Aquitaine (annulled 15 years later).

1182   Phillipe Auguste expels the Jews from France.

13th century

1209   Start of the Albigensian crusade against the Cathar heretics on Languedoc.

1214   Phillipe Auguste wins the provinces of Normandy and Anjou back from John of England.

1270   King Louis IX (St. Louis) dies on his way to the eighth crusade to the Holy Land.

14th Century

1309   Pope Clement V expelled from Rome. Sets up papal court at Avignon (until 1377).

1337   Start of the Hundred Years' War between the Plantaganets of England and the Capetians over who should rule France.

1360   Treaty of Brétigny cedes Aquitaine to England.

15th century

1415   Henry V of England invades France. Victory at Agincourt. He marries the daughter of Charles IV of France.

1429   Charles V of France mounts campaign against Henry V with Jeanne d'Arc.

1431   Jeanne d'Arc captured and burnt at the stake in Rouen. English driven from all French possession except Calais.

1475   Hundred Years' War is ended by the Treaty of Picquigny.

16th century

1515   Succession of François 1.

1539   Ordinance of Villers-Cotterêts creates 192 articles governing, among other things, the foundation of modern French law using French instead of Latin.

1541   Calvin publishes his 'Institutes of the Christian Religion'.

1562   Start of the Wars of Religion – a 36-year crisis between the Protestant Huguenots (including the Bourbons) and the Catholic League supported by Spain. It continues until 1598.

1570   Treaty of St. Germain – first efforts at peace.

1572   20,000 Huguenots killed at the St. Bartholomew's Day Massacre.

1589   King Henry III assassinated and succeeded by Henry IV – after his conversion to Catholicism in 1593 in order to assume the throne.

1598   Edict of Nantes guarantees the political and religious rights of Protestants and unites France.

17th century

1610   Henry IV assassinated. He is succeeded by Louis XIII with his mother Marie de Médicis as Regent. Towns are expanded, trade flourishes and St. Vincent de Paul starts pioneering work in social welfare.

1624   Cardinal Richelieu takes the reins of government, establishes absolute royal power and suppresses protestant influences. Start of the thirty years' war against the Hapsburgs under Charles V.

1635   Richelieu founds the Académie Française.

1642   Death of Richelieu (and Louis XIII). Cardinal Mazarin takes over. Louis XIV (The Sun King) succeeds as a minor.

1648   Peace of Westphalia ends the Thirty Years' War and Spain's dominance of European affairs. Alsace is confirmed as part of France and French is established as the language of diplomacy.

1662   Louis XIV attains his majority and decides to rule alone, drawing his ministers from the bourgeoisie and reducing the nobility to mere courtiers.

1672   Louis XIV moves his court to the newly converted 14,000 room palace of Versailles and gathers writers, playwrights, artists, musicians and philosophers.

1678   Peace of Nijmegen ends the war with Holland and absorbs Franche-Comté into France.

1685   Edict of Nantes is revoked and once again Catholicism is imposed on France. Protestants are persecuted.

18th century

1715   Louis XIV dies and is succeeded by Louis XV (aged 5) with the Duke of Orléans as Regent. Many of France's colonies are lost, and the court is corrupt and frivolous. Good economic policies help the country to prosper with better standards of living.

1766   Lorraine is absorbed into France.

1769   Corsica becomes part of France.

1774   Louis XVI becomes king. Lafayette takes part in the American War of Independence. The ideas of Voltaire, Rousseau, Montesquieu etc. attack the clergy and sow the seeds of revolution.

1783   First balloon flight by the Montgolfier brothers and rapid technological progress begins.

The French Revolution

1789–99   The Estates General renamed the National Assembly. The Bastille stormed. Privileges were abolished and Rights of Man declared.

1791   King and his wife, Marie Antoinette, and his children arrested in flight and suspended from office.

1792   Signing of the Convention. Prussians forced to retreat at Valmy. France is proclaimed a Republic (22 Sept.).

1793   Louis XVI executed. Execution of Marat.

1794   Execution of Robespierre and Danton. Directory of Five appointed to run the country.

1795   France adopted the metric system.

1799   Napoleon Bonaparte returns to Paris after a series of successful military campaigns against the Austrians and British, overthrows the Directory and declares himself First Consul.

The Empire
19th Century

1804   Napoleon is crowned Emperor by Pope Pius VII in Paris.

1805   Napoleon abandons his plan to invade England; Battle of Trafalgar gives Britain control of the seas. France wins battles of Ulm and Austerlitz.

1808   French troops bogged down in the Peninsular War.

1812   Napoleon invades Russia and is forced to retreat from Moscow.

1813   Battle of Leipzig; a victory for Prussia – they enter France.

1814   Paris falls to the Prussian Army.

The Restoration

1814   Napoleon abdicates at Fontainbleau (20 April) and retires to Elba.

Louis XVIII returns from exile in England.

1815   The Hundred Days – an attempt to re-establish the Empire. Napoleon marches north and meets the Allies under the Duke of Wellington at Waterloo; he is defeated and exiled to the island of St. Helena (He dies in 1821). Louis XVIII is restored to the throne. France returns to the frontiers of 1792.

The July Monarchy

1824   Charles X succeeds Louis XVIII.

1830   Ordinances de St. Cloud leads to an outbreak of revolution. Charles X is deposed, and Louis Philippe becomes king.

1837   First passenger train service opens between Paris and St. Germain-en-Laye.

Second Republic and Second Empire

1848   Monarchy overthrown and Louis Napoleon elected President of the Republic by universal suffrage.

1851   Louis Napoleon dissolves the legislative assembly and declares himself president for a ten-year term.

1852   Second Empire (with Napoleon III as Emperor) is declared.

1860   Savoy and Nice become part of France.

1870   War is declared on Prussia. Defeat at Sedan ends the Second Empire. Louis Napoleon is deposed and exiled.

The Republic

1870   Third Republic is proclaimed.

1871   German troops advance and Paris falls. Under the Treaty of Frankfurt, France gives up Alsace and part of Lorraine.

1884   Trade Unions recognized.

1885   Vaccination for rabies discovered by Pasteur.

1889   Inauguration of the Eiffel Tower in Paris.

1894   The Dreyfus Affair (forged evidence wrongly convicts a Jewish staff officer of spying).

20th century

1905   Separation of Church and State.

1914   Outbreak of First World War. German advance halted by the Battle of the Marne. Four years of trench warfare follow, resulting in massive loss of life on both sides.

1918   Armistice is signed on 11 Nov.

1919   Treaty of Versailles. Territories lost in 1871 restored to France.

1934   National Assembly is attacked by right-wing demonstrators.

1936   Léon Blum forms his Popular Front government.

1939   Outbreak of World War II.

1940   France is overrun by the German army. Armistice signed by Marshal Pétain. North and Atlantic seaboard occupied by Germans. Pro-German 'French State' established at Vichy.

1941   General de Gaulle forms Free French Forces and declares the Comité National Français to be the true French government in exile in London.

1944   June. The Allies land in Normandy. Paris is liberated by French troops under General de Gaulle.

1945   Armistice signed at Reims.

1946   The Fourth Republic is declared. Women have the vote. Proportional representation adopted. De Gaulle retires. Governments last an average of six months.

1954   Frances abandons her colonies in Indo-China. Morocco and Tunisia gain their independence.

1958   Algerian crisis leads to downfall of the Fourth Republic. Fifth Republic declared under de Gaulle. European Economic Community (EEC) comes into effect. New constitution (mostly written by de Gaulle) is voted in by referendum.

1962   Algerian independence.

1966   De Gaulle withdraws French troops from NATO. NATO headquarters moves to Brussels.

1968   Workers wanting better working conditions join students rioting for educational reforms. National Assembly dissolved. Gaullists win elections. De Gaulle's referendum in April is defeated. De Gaulle resigns.

1969   Gaullist Georges Pompidou is elected President.

1970   General de Gaulle dies.

1974   Valéry Giscard d'Estaing is elected President.

1981   François Mitterrand elected President. Inauguration of the TGV (train à grande vitesse) high speed train linking Paris, Lyon, Marseilles and Bordeaux.

1983   Mitterrand includes members of the Communist Party in his government.

1986   Emergence of the Front National (National Front) led by Jean Marie le Pen. Jacques Chirac becomes Prime Minister.

1988   François Mitterrand re-elected president with Edith Cresson as France's first woman Prime Minister (resigned 1992).

1995   Jacques Chirac elected President with Alain Juppé as Prime Minister.

1996   François Mitterrand dies.

1997   Juppé resigns after socialist victory in elections. Lionel Jospin appointed Prime Minister.

CULTURAL BRIEFING

Painting and Sculpture

12th–15th centuries

Although easel painting appeared in France in the 14th century, stained glass and sculpture were the main adornments of churches and cathedrals. With the arrival of Gothic architecture, larger areas of wall could be opened up and much more delicate glass could be used thanks to the new systems of leading and support, leaving less wall space for frescoes. The cathedrals of Chartres, Notre Dame de Paris, Evreux and the Sainte-Chapelle contain among the most famous and impressive examples of the art of stained glass. The art of manuscript illumination reached a climax in the 15th century when artists became free to provide books for private use (including the Book of Hours). One of the first French portraits was painted in 1350 ('Portrait of John the Good' – now in the Musée du Louvre) and the influence of Italian and Flemish painting can be seen in the works of the major artists of the 15th century – Jean Fouquet, Enguerrand Quarton and the Master of Moulins.

16th century

The court painters during the reign of Henry IV and the regency of Marie de Medici formed the second school of Fontainbleau. Among them were Toussaint Dubreuil, Ambroise Dubois and

Martin Fréminet. The 16th century also produced fine jewellery and articles of personal adornment – Etienne Delaune was one of the most famous goldsmiths of this period. The technique for painting enamel on copper was developed in Limoges during the reign of Louis XV, and Léonard Limosin was the leading exponent of the new art form.

Classicism

17th century

In the early part of the 17th century, Simon Vouet returned from Italy after a long stay and, together with his pupil Eustache le Sueur, breathed new life into French painting. In 1648 the Royal Academy of Painting and Sculpture was founded by Charles le Brun who, as the main court painter, dominated French painting until his death in 1690. Sculpture continued to show strong Italian influences, especially the work of Jacques Sarrazin whose studies in Rome gave his work a modern-classical style. Meanwhile, the work of François Anguier and his brother Michel showed more Baroque tendencies. Voltaire once said that French painting began with Nicholas Poussin, and he and Phillippe de Champaigne were at this time painting intellectual works that drew on philosophical, historical and theological themes. Nicolas Tournier and Georges de la Tour were both greatly influenced by the way the Italian painter Caravaggio used light and shade, and by his portrayal of ordinary people.

Baroque and Rococo

18th century

Most of the painters working in France at the turn of the century were heavily influenced by Flemish painting – Desportes, Largillière and Rigaud painted elaborate still lifes and heavy formal portraits. More popular were the works of Boucher, Watteau and Fragonard who painted 'fêtes gallantes', picnics and all manner of pastoral scenes with mythological overtones. The religious painters of this period (among them Charles le Fosse, Restout and a pupil of Le Brun, Antoine Coypel), reflected the less stoical ideals of the 18th century in their works while Nattier and Quentin de la Tour sparked a revival in portraiture. The Baroque influence was coursing through sculpture, and the Adam brothers, Cousteau and Slodtz, incorporated the Baroque style's expressiveness into their sculptures with their portrayal of sweeping garments and attention to detail. Bouchardon, on the other hand, had studied in Rome and his work continued in the classical tradition. Towards the end of the century, Jean-Baptiste Chardin brought the humble domesticity of Flemish painting to his simple still lifes. In the decorative arts, fashionable society created a demand for luxury furniture and the Vincennes Porcelain factory moved to Sèvres and began the production of luxury items. The deep blue known as 'Sèvres blue' originates from this period and craftsmen (among them Thomas Germain) were producing heavily ornamented Rococo (rocaille) gold and silver plates for the aristocratic tables of the time.

Neo-Classicism

At the end of the 18th century, the Royal Academy reacted against the elaborate and decorative style of the Baroque and returned to the classical style of painting and sculpture. Jacques-Louis David was a leading follower of this precise severe new classicism. His works contain themes of antique history, heroism and tragedy and he was made official state painter by Napoleon and produced enormous canvasses, including one of his coronation in 1804. In sculpture, artists tried to concentrate more on anatomical accuracy and drew on the Græco-Roman models for inspiration. Houdon was one of the greatest sculptors of the 18th century and his works included portrait busts of many of the famous names of the period including Voltaire, Buffon, Madame Adelaide, and the American presidents, Benjamin Franklin and George Washington.

The First Empire

19th century

The early part of the 19th century saw David and two of his pupils, A.J. Gros and A.L. Goridet-Trioson, receiving commissions from Napoleon to record the heroic events of the Empire. The painters of the day were a bit like troubadours – recording heroic events from the Empire's history.

The Second Empire and Romanticism

Of all David's pupils, Jean Auguste Dominique Ingres was the most famous. He continued to uphold the classical tradition, while another more romantic movement was gaining ground. Two friends, Gericault and Delacroix, led the Romantic Movement. Gericault's painting of the 'Raft of the Medusa' and Delacroix's painting of the 'July Revolution of 1830' illustrate perfectly this wildly dramatic style. Painters like Camille Corot and Jean-François Millet started to paint in the open air and they got together to form the Barbizon School. Their paintings drew inspiration from peasant life and simple rustic scenes. The works of Millet, in particular, represent a devout reverence for country life (his work would later exert a strong influence on Van Gogh).

Realism

The works of Millet anticipated the realism of Gustav Courbet, Daumier and Edouard Manet, who used realism to depict the life of Parisian middle classes while inserting many references to the Old Masters in his paintings.

Impressionism

This term derives from the title of a painting by Claude Monet 'Impression, Soleil Levant' (Impression: Sunrise) and was initially a term of derision. This school of painting painted from nature out of doors, using the ephemeral effects of light to capture fleeting images. Many of the Impressionists painted the same subject over and over at various times of day in order to capture the different impressions given by the altering light patterns. The Impressionists were led by Monet and included Alfred Sisley, Camille Pisarro, Berthe Morisot and Pierre-August Renoir.

Post-Impressionism

This term is applied to the works of both Paul Cézanne and Paul Gauguin, although their work is very different. Gauguin painted in a primitive style, mostly in Tahiti, while Cézanne painted in and around Avignon where his still lifes and, in particular, his landscapes lead towards cubism. Van Gogh also worked in the south of France and his vivid landscapes and still lifes were created using a technique that foreshadowed the work of Georges Seurat, who applied his paint in small dots or uniform brush strokes (Pointillism) to produce an image.

Paul Degas and Henri Toulouse-Lautrec both preferred working in the studio to the outdoors. Degas used his superb draughtsmanship to record his two favourite subjects, horse racing and the ballet, in sculpture as well as painting. Toulouse-Lautrec haunted the bars, brothels and music halls of Montmartre in Paris, recording the dancers and revellers there in a style that almost borders on the caricature. Although a contemporary of the Post-Impressionists, Henri Rousseau painted jungle and desert scenes as well as dreamy suburban scenes of Pairs in his own naïve style. Called 'Le Douanier' – he was a customs official – he only painted on Sundays.

Symbolism

The forerunners of the Symbolist painters were led by Gauguin, who moved to Pont-Aven (a favourite haunt of Corot in the 1860s) and founded the Pont-Aven School of painting with Emile Bernard and Paul Serusier. They favoured symbolic subjects and paved the way for the 'Nabis' group of painters who included Vuillard, Denis and Bonnard. This school of painting advocated the importance of colour over shape and meaning.

Sculpture in the early 19th century gave France a wealth of memorial sculptures. François Rude followed the heroic classical style, while Jean-Baptiste Carpeaux's more romantic works look back on the gaiety of the Baroque. Late 19th century sculpture was dominated by Auguste Rodin whose massive bronze and marble figures of men and women often intertwined and sometimes incomplete were much misunderstood during his lifetime. Among his best-known works are 'The Kiss' and 'The Thinker.' Rodin's most gifted pupil was Camille Claudel.

Avant-Garde Movements

20th century

Fauvism

The forerunner of abstract painting, the Fauvist painters (among them Marquet, Maurice de Vlaminck, André Derain and Henri Matisse – who later went on to develop his own personal exploration of colour) were remarkable for their arbitrary use of intensely bright colour. Their name derives from a derisory criticism of their work by a critic at the autumn salon of painting in 1905, who likened the artists to 'Wild Cats'.

Cubism

Although the early beginnings of cubism can be seen in the works of Cézanne, the movement was truly launched with the early works of Pablo Picasso, a Spaniard who made France his adopted home. The Cubists (who included F. Léger, Juan Gris and Georges Braque) deconstructed their subject matter into a series of layered and intersecting planes, often in a limited variety of colours. Collages created from cloth, string, pieces of newspaper, wool, hair, etc. were also a favourite medium of the cubists.

Surrealism

Dadaism was a literary and artistic revolutionary movement that started in Switzerland during World War I and grew into the Surrealist movement. During the 1920s and 1930s, surrealist painting gave new energy to the French artistic community. The subject matter was dreamy and irrational and incorporated, for the first time, symbolic images of the subconscious mind. Duchamp, Masson, Picabia and Magritte were all early leaders of this movement. Max Ernst was a German Dadaist painter working in Paris, whose work exerted a strong influence on the development of surrealism. The most famous surrealist of all, Salvador Dali, came relatively late to the movement.

Sculpture in the first half of the 20th century was dominated by Gustav Maillol whose voluptuous female figures owed more to formal analysis than to the influence of Rodin. Braque and Picasso also experimented with sculpture, and Marcel Duchamp created 'Objets Trouvés' ('Found Objects') – the most famous of which was a urinal which he signed and titled 'Fountain', thus causing a scandal when it was first exhibited. The Swiss-born sculptor Alberto Giacometti was part of the surrealist movement in the 1930s and he went on to create the emaciated bronze figures for which he is famous.

Abstract Art

The new young generation of geometric Abstract painters was greatly influenced by a work by Herbin entitled 'Non-figurative, Non-objective Art.' Herbin's works since the 1950s have all been patterns of letters and geometric shapes in simple pure colours. Lyrical abstract artists focus on the study of texture and colour and painters like Riopelle and Mathieu applied their paint with a knife or directly from the tube. Soulages produced works influenced by the orient while Nicholas de Stael's work is a link between abstract and figurative painting.

New Realism

Pierre Restany is the leading painter of this early form of 'Pop Art' which attempted to portray the reality of consumerism in daily life. Other painters who worked to express energy and space through the new realism were Yves Klein and Dubuffet (whose later paintings and sculptures consist of puzzles made up of coloured or black and white units).

In sculpture, Arman took industrial items, broke them up and exhibited the compressed results, while César (who, among other things, created the statuette 'OSCAR' for the Hollywood Academy of Motion Picture awards) embedded broken-up symbols of society in glass.

Support-Surface Movement

Post 1960

Artists (among them Claude Viallet and Daniel Dezeuze) focused on the material state of the canvas and the way in which the paint was applied. Often, canvases would be removed from their stretchers cut up or folded.

In the 1980s, a more traditional approach to painting can be seen in the work of artists like Gérard Garouste and Jean-Charles Blais, and today the contemporary arts scene in France reflects a wide range of influences and styles.

Architecture

Prehistoric

Between 4000 and 2400 BC, stone megaliths were erected mainly in Brittany, although there are some to be found in the northern Languedoc and on Corsica.

Gallo-Roman

2nd century – 6th century BC

From the 1st century BC, the Romans built aqueducts, marketplaces, amphitheatres, temples, triumphal arches and bathhouses all over

France. The most impressive structures that remain are to be found in the south – especially on the coastal plains of Languedoc and in Provence. The Pont du Gard, between Nîmes and Avignon, is a fine example of Roman architectural brilliance. Well preserved remains of public buildings are also to be found in Nîmes, Arles and Orange.

The Dark Ages

(Merovingian and Carolingian)

6th century – 11th century

Most of the churches built during this period have either been destroyed or have been built over, as in the church of St. Denis (north of Paris) and in the Abbey of St. Germain in Auxerre. In the 9th century architecture returned to its Imperial classical influences, as in Aix la Chapelle and the oratory of Germigny-des-Près.

Romanesque

11th – 12th centuries

During the 11th century, religion experienced a revival and many churches were built in the 'Roman' style. The architects adapted existing buildings with Gallo-Roman vaulting and added rounded arches and heavy walls. There was little ornamentation and the buildings were simple and austere. Many of these churches were built for the pilgrims en route to Santiago de Compostela in Spain, and Romanesque abbeys can be found at Caen and all along the pilgrimage route. The Romanesque style continued in France until well into the 12th century.

Gothic

12th – 15th centuries

Northern France attained great wealth in the 12th century and was able to attract the finest architects, engineers, masons, and sculptors in order to build the grandest cathedrals in Europe. The Gothic style incorporated tall slender archways, ribbed vaults and constructed chapels along the side aisles. In the later Gothic buildings, the roofs were supported by flying buttresses on the exterior of the building. Gothic architecture became more and more ornate and the cathedrals of Chartres, Reims and Amiens are the most perfect examples of this period. In the 14th century Rayonnant Gothic (so called because of the delicate tracing of the rose windows with their 'Radiant' stained glass) gave France the Sainte Chapelle in Paris. By the end of the 15th century the decorative style had become even more lacy and flamboyant – 'Flamboyant Gothic'. The Clocher Neuf ('new bell tower') at Chartres, the Tour de Beurre at Rouen Cathedral and the Cathedral in Strasbourg are all typical examples of Flamboyant Gothic.

Renaissance

15th – 17th centuries

The Renaissance began in Italy in the early 15th century but it only really began to replace Gothic architecture in France towards the end of the 15th century. To begin with, Renaissance architecture, with its return to classical Roman and Greek forms, was combined with gothic ornamentation. It was in the building of the chateaux of the Loire Valley that the first signs of a move away from medieval tradition could be seen. During the reign of François I (1515–47), building in the Loire Valley reached its peak with the construction of many chateaux, and the preoccupation with Italianate is much in evidence. The French architectural tradition of corner towers, irregular roofs and dormer windows is combined with monumental indoor staircases and ornate decoration.

Mannerism

Work on the Chateau de Fontainbleau began in 1527 under the direction of Gilles de Breton. Gothic churches continued to be built in France throughout the 16th century.

Baroque

17th century

> Three architects – Jacques Lemercier, François Mansart and Louis le Vau – were primarily responsible for setting the standards of French classical architecture. Le Vau was the first architect to work on the Palace of Versailles for Louis XIV. Mansart built the Château du Balleroy and the Château de Masions-Lafitte and his plan for a central pavilion with projecting wings, incorporating Doric, Ionic and Corinthian columns along the facades, profoundly influenced French palatial architecture. Lemercier supported the Italian style and le Vau is also known for his town houses for the nobility (Hotel de Lambert in Paris, for example) which he built in the grandiose style characteristic of the classical style of Louis XIV. He also built the Château de Vaux-le-Vicomte. Jules Hardouin-Mansart (le Vau's successor at Versailles) designed the Église de Dôme – considered to be the finest church in France.

Neo-Classicism

18th century

> France's greatest Neo-classical architect was Jacques-Germain Soufflot (who designed, among other things, the Panthéon in Paris). The style, employing Greek and Roman architectural forms, was used extensively by the Emperor Napoleon in the building of monumental constructions intended to glorify the achievements of imperial France. Among the many examples of Neo-classical architecture to be seen in Paris are the Arc de Triomphe, the church of La Madeleine, the façade of the Palais Bourbon, the Arc de Carousel at the Louvre, the Assemblée Nationale and the Bourse. Later in the century, the interiors of French palaces became more intimate, and boudoirs and small salons were ornately furnished and decorated. The Hôtel de Soubise by Delamair and the Hotel Matignon by Courtonne (both in Paris) are examples of this new 'Rocaille' style.

19th century

In the early 19th century, as Napoleon oversaw the construction of his monumental buildings, the Neo-classical style was gradually dying out and the movement known as historicism was becoming popular. This movement harked back to historical architectural styles, such as those used in medieval buildings and churches. The 'Monuments Historiques' (a society for the classification and preservation of historic buildings) was founded in 1830 and the trend was supported enthusiastically by Violet le Duc, whose efforts to restore as much as possible of France's architectural heritage can be seen to this day in buildings all over the country.

Town planning was an important feature of 19th century France and Baron Hausmann, Préfet of the Département of the Seine, laid down the principals of the public works programme that would modernise Paris. A similar programme was undertaken in Lyons. In the late 19th century many public edifices were constructed for the Universal Exhibitions that were held in Paris, amongst them the Eiffel Tower, the Grand-Palais and the Point Alexandre. In the 1890s the Art Nouveau architects, influenced by their contemporaries in England and Belgium, were creating buildings that were designed as a whole – exteriors, interiors, decorations and even furniture were all co-ordinated in one homogeneous style. Hector Guimard was the chief proponent of this style in France, designing, among other things, the world famous entrances to the metro stations. Another example of public Art Nouveau building in Paris was the Gare d'Orsay (now a museum).

20th century

The Stijl movement of architecture grew out of a reaction to Art Nouveau and other trends of the 19th century. The most perfect example of the simple geometric buildings built at this time is the Theatre de Champs-Elysées, constructed by the Perret Brothers with sculptural decoration by Bourdelle. In the first half of the century, architecture in France underwent a revival with the work of le Corbusier. He was a radical modernist and tried to adapt buildings to their function while considering the requirements of the human beings that would live and work in them. Of his many town developments, the Cité Radieuse in Marseilles and his chapel at Ronchamp in eastern France are among the most important works of modern architecture in France. Architects and sculptors sometimes work together in attempts to modify the urban landscapes and a recent project of this kind is Cergy-Pontoise, northwest of Paris – a collaboration between Ricardo Boffil and D. Karavan. President Pompidou commissioned the Centre Beaubourg in 1977 which was heavily criticised at the time, and his successor, Valéry Giscard d'Estaing, was instrumental in the Gare d'Orsay's transformation from railway station to museum. Recent innovative architectural projects have included the glass pyramid at the Louvre by I. M. Pei, the Grande Arche at La Défense, the Science Park and Museum at La Villette and the new Finance Ministry at Bercy. The Bibliothèque Nationale (National Library) is housed in a controversial new structure. France had a new cathedral consecrated in 1995 in Evry – a new town 20 km south of Paris. It was designed by the architect Mario Botta and cost 65m. French Francs.

Literature

Middle Ages

11th century

The 'Chanson de Roland' is thought to be the first work of literature in the French language. It is an epic poem by an unknown author recounting the heroic death of Charlemagne's nephew, Roland, who was ambushed on his way back from a crusade against the Muslims in 778.

Lyric poems of courtly love were composed and set to music by troubadours and their romantic tradition drew heavily on the Celtic legends such as King Arthur and the Knights of the Round Table and their quest for the Holy Grail, and the legend of Tristan and Iseult. Guillaume de Lorris and Jean de Meung wrote a 22,000 line poem called 'Roman de la Rose' that used allegorical figures like Shame and Fear, Pleasure and Riches to narrate the story. Among the other works from this period are the 'Ballades de Femmes du Temps Jadis' (Ballad of the Dead Women), a book of poems written by François Villon who was banished from France after stabbing a lawyer.

Renaissance

16th century

The 16th century was a turning point in French literature. La Pléiade, Rabelais and Montaigne were all writing during this period. François Rabelais wrote a huge rambling epic farce recounting the adventures of Gargantua, a mythical giant, and his son Pantagruel and encompassing every kind of person, language and event to be found in the France of the day. Montaigne wrote a series of essays on wide ranging topics and la Pléiade was part of a group of poets that included Pierre de Rosnay. Meanwhile Marie de la Fayette wrote what is considered to be the first major French novel, 'La Princesse de Clèves'.

Classicism

17th century

The Academie Française was founded in 1638 and with it the academic standards of French language, literature, grammar, spelling and rhetoric were strictly codified and regulated. The 17th century is known as the golden age of French literature ('Le Grand Siècle'). The theatre was transformed by the comedies of Molière – an actor who became the most popular playwright of his time – and by the tragedies of Pierre Corneille and Jean Racine who drew their subject matter from history and classical mythology. Poetry produced the exquisite verses of François de Malherbe and Jean de la Fontaine popularized the Fables of Aesop.

The Enlightenment

18th century

Philosophers dominated the literature of the 18th century. Jean-Jacques Rousseau – a convert to Catholicism who originally came from Switzerland – always considered himself a religious exile and in his sensitive writings about landscapes we can see the beginnings of romanticism. Voltaire wrote philosophical tales, arguing in his political works that society is fundamentally against nature, although his most famous work, 'Candide', ironically tells the story of a simple soul making the best of things despite the many problems that befall him. These works had a profound effect on Rousseau and in his 'Les Confessions' he asserts his own individuality and creates what is effectively the first modern autobiography.

Romantic Movement

19th century

The Romantic Movement was coloured by a new sense of preoccupation with the self and the emotions. Early exponents of the Romantic Movement were Madame de Staël, François-René de Chateaubriand and Benjamin Constant but it was Victor Hugo who became the key figure in French romantic literature. His novels 'Les Misérables' and 'Notre Dame de Paris' (The Hunch back of Notre Dame) were widely acclaimed and his poetry and plays are works of technical virtuosity, which are still revered in France and all over the world today. When he died in 1885, it is believed that 2m. people followed his funeral procession. Many of the most internationally famous works of French literature date from the 19th century. Stendhal gave us 'Le Rouge et le Noir'. Honoré de Balzac's vast series of novels known as 'La Comédie Humaine' covered just about every aspect of French society and illustrated all aspects of human behaviour. Aurore Dupain, who used the male pseudonym of Georges Sand, wrote about social injustice and romantic love in her novels while Alexandre Dumas the elder gave us the adventure stories of the 'Count of Monte Cristo' and 'The Three Musketeers'. In the middle of the 19th century, two writers were tried for immorality. Gustav Flaubert wrote a novel about an unfaithful wife, 'Madame Bovary', and Charles Baudelaire tried to publish his book of poems 'Les Fleurs du Mal'. Flaubert won his case and Madame Bovary was published without any cuts but Baudelaire lost his and although he had to cut several poems from the book, his poetry has endured to influence not only most of the poetry written in the late 19th century but also subsequent generations of French poets. Baudelaire also translated literature into French and was responsible for introducing the works of the American writer, Edgar Allan Poe, into France.

Symbolism

The aim of this movement was to express states of mind rather than recount stories of daily life. The creators of this movement, Paul Verulaine and Stephanie Mallarmé, were joined in their endeavours by Arthur Rimbaud who wrote 'Illuminations' and 'Une Saison en Enfer'.

Naturalism

Emil Zola claimed that he got the inspiration for his form of naturalism from the writings of Flaubert. He aimed to apply a scientific theory to the writing of novels and his main work, the 'Les Rougon-Macquart' series of novels, is the testament to his attempts.

20th century

The early part of the 20th century was dominated by Marcel Proust. His largely autobiographical novel, 'A la Recherche du Temps Perdu' (Remembrance of Things Past), examines in minute detail the recovery of past experiences from the unconscious mind and explores their true meaning. It remains one of the most important works of literature in the French language.

Surrealism

French literature was driven by surrealism until the outbreak of World War II. André Breton was the leader of this group of writers and he and the group published three manifestos on the subject. Other writers of the group included Guillaume Apollinaire (who is credited with the first use of the word 'Surrealism'), Paul Eluard and Louis Aragon (who wrote the famous surrealist work 'Le Paysan de Paris'). At the same time, Colette was writing her titillating novels recounting the early sexual exploits of schoolgirl heroines and managed to shock the more moralistic French readers. She later wrote a book about the German occupation of Paris called 'Paris de ma Fenêtre' (Paris from my Window).

Post World War II

Jean Paul Sartre was at the centre of the Existentialist group, perhaps the most significant movement to emerge after World War II. Together with Simone de Beauvoir and Albert Camus, he worked and frequented the cafés of Saint Germain des Près in Paris. All three writers were politically committed and stressed the need for this in their work. Camus' best known work, 'L'Étranger' (The Outsider), was nominated for the Nobel Prize for Literature in 1957. Simone de Beauvoir was the author of a ground-breaking study of women, 'The Second Sex', which has profoundly influenced feminist thinking to this day. Sartre wrote the manifesto of existentialism and his book 'L'Être et le Néant' (Being and Nothingness) maintains that existence has no inherent meaning or useful value.

1950s and 1960s

The writers of the 'Nouveau Roman' (New Novel) were challenging their readers by abandoning accepted narrative techniques and tackling subject matter previously considered too mundane and boring to be of merit. The main authors of this loosely knit group were Alain Robbe-Grillet and Nathalie Sarraute. Also at this time, the appearance of an extremely erotic novel called 'l'Histoire d'O', by Dominique Aury (published under a pseudonym), sold more copies than any other contemporary French novel outside France.

1980s

The Academie Française elected its first woman member, Marguerite Yourcenar (best known for her historical novels) in 1980, and in 1984 Marguerite Duras won the prestigious Prix Goncourt for her novel 'L'Amant' (The Lover). She also wrote the screenplay for, among other films, 'Hiroshima Mon Amour'. In recent years, French authors who have enjoyed popular success both in France and abroad include Françoise Sagan, Patrick Mondiano, Pascal Quignard and Denis Tillinac. The French reading public has always enjoyed a detective story and the books of Georges Simenon (starring Inspecteur Maigret) are widely read. So too are the 'roman policier' of Frédéric Dard (alias San Antonio), Léo Malet and Daniel Pennac.

Music

Troubadours and Minstrels

10th–13th centuries

The Troubadours in the south of France and the Trouvères in the north were travelling musicians. Their songs consisted of myths and legends and historical sagas. Their standing in society ranged from street singer to court musician. The Jongleurs were a group of musicians based in Paris belonging to a Guild whose controls were still in force up until the 18th century.

Harmonists and Theorists

12th–13th centuries

Franco of Cologne wrote the earliest treatise on the notation of fixed time values. Three composers and organists of Notre Dame de Paris, Léonin, Pérotin and Robert de Sabilon, active during the 11th and 12th centuries, helped to develop the art of musical notation. There were a large number of English music students in Paris during the 13th century, prompting much interaction between the composers from both countries. During the early 13th century, Paris was the centre of theoretical and practical musical experiment.

The Ars Nova

13th–14th centuries

Ars Nova was a style of music that began in Italy but spread rapidly to France. The old stiff rhythm styles were overturned by a freer approach to the melodic line. Phillippe de Vitry, poet, bishop and composer, wrote a treatise on the subject, and Machaut, who was a poet writing his own music, developed Vitry's principles. In the early 14th century, the work of Johannes de Muris, a close friend of Vitry and supporter of Ars Nova, was famous all over Europe. During the reigns of Charles V (1364–1380) and Charles VI (1380–1422), French music blossomed. France was the European musical centre during this period, under the influences of the University of Paris and the flowering of French gothic architecture.

The Huguenot Influence

15th–16th centuries

As well as contributing to the growth of polyphonic music (reaching its height in England with the works of Byrd, etc.), the Calvinist and Huguenot tradition of singing psalms produced settings by composers like Guillaume Franc and Calde le Jeune. Goudmiel Bourgeois was a Calvinist who lived in Geneva for much of his life and wrote fine choral settings of church music as well as psalm settings.

Early Keyboard Music

17th–early 18th centuries

The first French composer to write music specifically for the harpsichord was Chambonnières and he is known as the founder of the French Harpsichord School. He inspired a generation of composers like Dandrieu, Daquin, Rameau and, perhaps most famously, François Couperin ('The Great'). Both these composers were the contemporaries of Johann Sebastian Bach (writing in Germany) and Bach's keyboard music reflects influences from Couperin's music.

Early Opera

French opera, although initially influenced by Italian opera, followed its own course. The two principal composers of this period were Lully (in the late 17th century) and Rameau (in the early 18th century). The court of Louis XIV was a centre of culture and promoted the development and composition of music of all kinds including opera and ballet, with Lully as his court musician.

Orchestral Developments

18th century

In the 18th century A.D. Phildor established a series of concerts known as the 'Concerts Spirituels' (Spiritual Concerts) and these had a profound effect on the development of French orchestral music. The clarinet made its first appearance in the orchestration for a Rameau opera and the repertoire of the symphonic orchestra was greatly enriched by Stamitz (who was composing and conducting at Mannheim) and Gossec (who is looked upon as the father of the symphony in France).

A group of 'savants' known as the 'Encyclopedists' were compiling the great 'French Encyclopaedia'. Among them were Diderot and d'Alembert, whose writings on music remain among the most important works of reference for the study of 18th century music.

Composers writing during this period include Monsigny, Grétyr, Lesueur and Méhul. The Paris Conservatoire of Music was founded in Paris in 1784 and the 'Prix de Rome', that to this day sends talented young composers to work at the Villa Medici, dates from 1803.

Romantic Music

19th century

During the 19th century, the principal French composers were Boiledieu, Auber and Halévy, who all composed operas. Meanwhile, the art of the violin was being developed by Kreutzer (who wrote many advanced technical studies for the instrument), Baillot and Rode.

Hector Berlioz was the most famous of late 19th century French composers. He wrote in an adventurous and innovative style much criticised at the time and left a legacy of symphonies, choral music and oratorio. Other outstanding composers of the period were Gounod, Delibes, Bizet, Chabrier, Massenet, Charpentier and Vidor.

19th and early 20th centuries

The Société Nationale was founded in Paris in 1870 to promote orchestral music and fight the national obsession with operatic music. The organization was supported by many of the French composers writing during this period, including César Franck (who incorporated influences from Bach, Beethoven and Wagner into his music), d'Indry, Saint-Saëns and Fauré. The group of composers known as the 'Schola Cantorum' was founded by another pupil of Franck, Vincent d'Indry, with the purpose of elevating French church music. It did a great deal to encourage contemporary composers, among them Duparc, Dukas, Magnard and Sévérac. At the same time, another group of composers, led by

Debussy and including Ravel, Floret Schmitt and Roussel, was active. A third movement consisted of Saint-Saëns and Fauré. Perhaps the most modernistic of the French composers writing at this time was Satie, who wrote whimsical works, mostly for keyboard.

1920s and 1930s

After World War I, French composition was dominated by a group of musicians known as 'Les Six' (The Six). Consisting of Honnegar, Milhaud, Tailleferre, Durey, Auric and Poulenc, they often wrote in styles that reacted against the styles of Debussy and Ravel.

World War II

During the occupation of France by Germany, the musical institutions were under German control and very little French music was either produced or performed. However, the director of French radio organised some festival programmes of French music with works by French composer such as Berlioz, Lalo, Chabrier, Saint-Saëns and Fauré. From 1943, a society known as 'La Pléiade' in Paris also gave private concerts of music by French composers. There was also an underground organization, the National Committee of Musicians, which united musicians, circulated secretly published literature and gave performances of banned works by French, Jewish, Russian and British composers. In the years immediately after World War II, the principal composers were René Leibowitz (who was a pupil of the pioneer of the twelve-tone scale, Schönberg), Olivier Messiaen (best known for his organ music) and Pierre Boulez.

Contemporary Music

Jazz hit Paris in the 1920s and has remained popular with the French ever since. France has contributed the talents of the violinist Stefan Grapelli to the world of jazz, and, more recently, the pianists Martial Solal and Michel Petrucciani. The Chanson

Française is the most widespread and popular form of French music, with traditions that go back to the troubadours. The songs have remained to this day an important medium for imparting ideals and protests as well as romantic stories. Some of the most famous singers of these songs have been Charles Trenet, Georges Brassens, Jacques Brel and, most famous of all, Edith Piaf.

Although France has remained culturally very centralized, in recent years, regional schools of music have sprung up in 38 towns in France and the provinces are enjoying a much richer musical life. In 1966 a Bureau de Musique was established within the Ministry of Cultural Affairs and government subsidies are given to some 35 orchestras around France. The Bureau also encourages the broadcast of music and has instituted courses for elementary school teachers in new methods of musical instruction. There are also many 'Lycées Musicaux' which offer specialized musical tuition – as well as the normal general education – to talented pupils.

Cinema

1890s–World War I

The Lumière Brothers invented the 'moving pictures' and in 1895 the world's first public screening of this new art form took place in the Grand Café on the boulevard des Capucines in Paris. The Lumière Brothers concentrated on news and documentaries. Pre-First World War movies in France were dominated by Charles Pathé.

1920s & 1930s

French film began to develop along avant-garde experimental lines with the work of Jean Renoir (son of Auguste, the impressionist painter), Marcel Carné and René Clair. Among the leading actors of the 1930s Jean Gabin was perhaps the most internationally famous.

New Wave

The French film industry went dormant during and just after World War II but in the late 1950s a new generation of directors sprung up. They were dubbed the New Wave or 'Nouvelle Vague'. The directors that made up this group – Jean-Luc Godard, François Truffaut, Claude Chabrol, Eric Rohmer, Jacques Rivette, Louis Malle and Alain Renais being the principal names – made very different kinds of films but they were united by a common belief that all creative decisions should be made by the film maker and not dictated by commercial considerations – thus the term 'Film d'Auteur' (the author's film). In 1956, Roger Vadim's 'Et Dieu Créa la Femme' (And God Created Woman) catapulted Brigitte Bardot to stardom and started a youth culture created around the little fishing village of St. Tropez in the Côte d'Azur. 'L'Année Dernière à Marienbad' (Last Year at Marienbad, Alain Renais 1961), 'Les Quatre Cents Coups' (The 400 Blows, François Truffaut 1959) and 'A Bout du Souffle' (Breathless, Jean-Luc Godard, 1960) were a few of the triumphs of French cinema during the 1960s. Many world famous stars came out of the French cinema of this period, including Catherine Deneuve, Fernandel, Maurice Chevalier, Alain Delon, Jean-Pierre Cassel and Jean-Paul Belmondo. Jacques Tati was an actor/director also working at this time, and his humorous movies about the bungling M. Hulot have become comedy classics.

Contemporary Cinema

French cinema has acquired a reputation for being 'arty' and elitist but many of its films have received worldwide acclaim and popular support. The best known directors working during the 1980s and 1990s number Jean-Jacques Beinex ('Diva', 1981 and 'Betty Blue', 1986), Luc Besson ('Subway', 1985; 'The Big Blue', 1988; 'Nikita', 1990; and 'Leon', 1994). Claude Berri created 'Jean de Florette' (1986) followed by the equally popular sequel 'Manon des

Sources'. The 1980s gave rise to a generation of tough male actors like Jean Reno (Subway and The Big Blue) and Richard Bohrenger (Diva) while in the 1990s, Daniel Auteuil (Manon des Sources), Hippolyte Gardot (Un Monde sans Pitié) and Fabrice Lucchini (La Discrète, Beaumarchais) have been popular. Perhaps the most well-known of today's French actors is Gérard Depardieu who has become internationally famous through his appearances in American as well as French films over the last 20 years. His French cinematic successes include 'Jean de Florette', 'Cyrano de Bergerac' and 'Le Dernier Métro'. Contemporary French film actresses include Emmanuelle Béart, Sandrine Bonnaire, Carole Bouquet and, perhaps more internationally famous, Juliette Binoche and Isabelle Adjani. The French film industry hosts the most famous and prestigious of all the international film festivals each year at Cannes. The top prize, the 'Palme d'Or' is one of the most sought-after cinematic awards. In 1976 the French movie industry instituted the 'Césars' – its own version of the Hollywood 'Oscars' – to reward its directors, actors and technicians.

MAJOR CITIES

The international code for telephoning or faxing France is the code required to dial out of your own country followed by 33.

PARIS:

Paris is the commercial, financial, and industrial focus of France, a major transportation hub and a cultural and intellectual centre of international renown. A fishing village when it was conquered in

52 BC by Caesar, it became an important Roman town. It was a
Merovingian capital throughout the 5th century and became the
national capital with the accession in 987 of Hugh Capet, Count of
Paris. It flowered as the centre of medieval commerce and scholasti-
cism but suffered severely during the Hundred Years' War. Paris
consistently displayed a rebellious and independent spirit, as is
shown in its resistance to Henry IV (1589–93); the first Fronde
(1648–49); the revolutions of 1789, 1830 and 1848; and the Commune
of Paris (1871). During World War II it was occupied (1940–44) by the
Germans but was, miraculously, relatively undamaged.

The Seine River runs through Paris. On its stately, formal Right
Bank are many of the most fashionable streets and shops, and such
landmarks as the Arc de Triomphe, place de la Concorde, Louvre,
and Sacré Coeur. The Left Bank (La Rive Gauche) houses govern-
mental offices and is the site of much of the city's intellectual life.
The Rive Gauche is known for its old Latin Quarter and for such
landmarks as Paris' main University, La Sorbonne, the Luxembourg
Palace, the Panthéon, and the modern Pompidou Art Centre
(Beaubourg). The historic core of Paris is the Île de la Cité, a small
island occupied in part by the Palais de Justice and the Cathedral
of Notre Dame de Paris. Above the city rises the Eiffel Tower. Paris is
divided into 20 arrondissements (boroughs) and is governed by a
mayor.

TRANSPORT

Airports

Aéroport de Roissy-Charles de Gaulle: Tel: (0)1 48-62-22-80.
Most international transatlantic flights land at this airport. Terminal 2
serves Air France and affiliates. It is connected to Paris via either
train or bus. RER B3 (a Parisian commuter train service) goes to the

Gare du Nord (a mainline Paris railway station) where you can connect to the Metro system. Roissy-bus (Tel: (0)1 48-04-18-24) stops
outside the American Express office at the Rue du Scribe in central
Paris. Air France buses go to and from Roissy at regular intervals from
several locations in the city Tel: (0)1 41-56-89-00.

Aéroport d'Orly: Tel: (0)1 49-75-15-15.
Used by many charters and continental flights. Connected to Paris by
Orly-rail, a shuttle bus that takes passengers to the Orly RER C3
(Paris commuter service) train station. Or take the Jetbus to the
Ville-Louis Aragon Metro stop. Air France buses run between Orly
and several central Paris locations Tel: (0)1 41-56-89-00.

Trains

French railways are operated by SNCF, Tel: (0)8 36-35-35-35
(reservations and information).

Paris has 6 railway stations, each divided into Grandes Lignes
(long-distance trains) and Banlieue (suburban trains). Tickets can be
bought at travel agencies or from ticket machines (billieterie) at the
stations and must be validated using the machines at the entrance to
the platform before boarding the train.

Gare du Nord: Trains to and from northern France, Britain (including
Eurostar), the Netherlands, Scandinavia, the Commonwealth of
Independent States, northern Germany.

Gare de l'Est: Trains to and from eastern France, Luxembourg, parts
of Switzerland (Basle, Zürich, Lucerne), southern Germany, Austria
and Hungary.

Gare de Lyon: Trains to and from southern and southeastern France,
parts of Switzerland (Geneva, Lausanne, Berne), Italy, Greece.

Gare d'Austerlitz: Trains to and from the Loire valley, southwestern
France, Spain and Portugal.

Gare St. Lazare: Trains to and from Normandy.

Gare Montparnasse: Trains to and from Brittany and part of southwest France.

CITY TRANSPORT

Buses

Most international buses arrive at the Gare Routiere Internationale de Paris-Gallieni.

The city bus service is slower and more expensive than the metro system. Tickets can be used on either buses or Metro and can be bought either in the metro stations or on the bus.

Paris public transport is run by RATP (Régie Autonome Transports Parisiens) Tel: (0)1 40-06-71-44 (Bureau de Tourisme RATP).

Passes can be bought for unlimited travel on buses and metro for 3 or 5 days. Paris Visite passes are valid for travel buses, metros and RER and also offer discounts on various tourist attractions; services can be bought at airports, metro and RER stations.

Metro

Paris has an efficient and inexpensive metro (underground) system that has been operating since 1898. It is run by RATP (Tel: (0)1 40-06-71-44 Bureau de Tourism). Stations are marked **M**. Tickets can be bought either singly or in 'carnets' (books) of 10 from ticket booths on metro stations.

Taxis

Taxis operate 24 hours and can either be hailed, found on designated taxi stands, train stations, etc. or by telephone.
(Radio cabs)
Alpha Taxis: Tel: (0)1 45-85-85-85.

Taxis Radio Etoile: Tel: (0)1 41-27-27-27.

Taxis G7: Tel: (0)1 47-39-47-39.

Taxis Bleue: Tel: (0)1 49-36-10-10.

Taxis 7000: Tel: (0)1 42-70-00-42.

Scooter and Bicycle Hire

La Maison du Vélo: 11 rue Fénelon, 10ième. Tel: (0)1 42-81-24-72.
Metro Poissonière.

   Agence Contact Location: (Motorcycles and scooters) 24 rue Arc de Triomphe, 17ème. Tel: (0)1 47-66-19-19. Metro Etoile.

TRAVELLERS INFORMATION

Tourist Offices

Bureau d'Accueil Central: 127 avenue des Champs-Elysées, 8eme. Tel: (0)1 49-52-53-54.
Metro Charles-de-Gaulle-Etoile
Central Tourist Information Telephone Line: (0)1 49-52-53-56.
Office also at Gare du Nord Tel: (0)1 45-26-94-82 and Gare de Lyon Tel: (0)1 43-43-33-24; and at Aéroport de Roissy-Charles-de-Gaulle Tel: (0)1 48-62-27-29, Aéroport d'Orly Sud Tel: (0)1 49-75-00-90, Aéroport d'Orly Ouest Tel: (0)1 49-75-01-39.

Information Websites

www.mairie-paris.fr www.franceguide.com (tourist information)
www.business-travel-net.com (business travel information)
www.iti.fr (route planner)
www.autoroutes.fr (information autoroutes)
www.equipmewnt.gouv.fr (roads and traffic information)
www.afp.com (French and international news)
www.sytadin.tm.fr (Paris traffic reports)
Email: info@mdlf.co.uk

Consulates
See page 161.

Financial and Currency
American Express: 11 rue Scribe, 9ème. Tel: (0)1 47-77-77-07.
Fax: (0)1 47-77-74-57.
  Metro Opera or Auber.
  Currency exchange available at cash ATMs throughout Paris and at railway stations etc.

Emergency
Fire: Tel: 18
Police: Tel: 17

Medical Emergency
(Ambulance): Tel: 15 Outside Paris: (0)1 45-67-50-50.

Hospitals
Hôpital Franco-Britannique de Paris, 3 rue Barbès.
Tel: (0)1 46-39-22-22. Metro Anatole France.
Hôpital Américain de Paris. 63 boulevard Victor Hugo, Neuilly.
Tel: (0)1 46-41-25-25. Metro Porte-Maillot then bus #82.
  Pharmacies. Each Arrondissment has 'pharmacie de garde' (pharmacy on call) information posted on each pharmacy door.

Internet Access
Café Orbital: 13 rue de Médicis, 6ème. Tel: (0)1 43-25-76-77.
Web: www.orbital.fr email: info@orbital.fr Metro Odéon.

WebBar: 23 rue Picardy, 3ème. Tel: (0)1 42-72-66-55.
Web: www.webbar.fr email: webbar@webbar.fr
Metro République

Le Jardin de l'Internet. 79 boulevard St-Michel, 5ème.

Tel: (0)1 44-07-22-20. Web: perso.wanadoo.fr/jardin.internet

email: jardin-net@wanadoo.fr

Hotel Reservations

See central reservation numbers on page 155.

Car Hire

See central reservation numbers on page 156.

Landmarks

Cathédrale de Notre Dame de Paris: Tel: (0)1 42-34-56-10. Metro Cité.
Situated on the Ile de La Cité (the heart of Paris and the point from
which distances in and around Paris are measured), Notre Dame de
Paris is one of the greatest of France's cathedrals. Joan of Arc's trial
for heresy took place here and Victor Hugo was inspired by it to write
'The Hunchback of Notre Dame'.

Arc de Triomphe and Avenue des Champs-Elysées

Tel: (0)1 55-37-73-77. Metro Charles-de-Gaulle-Etoile.
The Arc de Triomphe was built by Napoleon and stands at the apex of
the Avenue des Champs Elysées commemorating France's military
victories. The eternal flame has marked the tomb of the Unknown
Soldier since 1920. The Avenue des Champs Elysées is a 10-lane tree
lined avenue, flanked by cafés and restaurants and terminates in the
Place de la Concorde. It is the most famous of the 12 avenues that
radiate outwards from the Arc de Triomphe.

La Tour Eiffel. Tel: (0)1 44-11-23-44. Web: www.tour-eiffel.fr
Metro Bir Hakeim.
Perhaps the most famous of European landmarks, the Eiffel Tower
was built in 1889 as the centrepiece of the Universal Exposition. It
has since served as a communications tower (especially during both

world wars) and is now France's most visited tourist attraction. On 5
April 1997 (1,000 days before the turn of the millennium) a countdown
clock was placed on the Seine side of the tower.

Musée du Louvre: Tel: (0)1 40-20-50-50. Web: www.louvre.fr
Metro Palais Royale/Musée du Louvre.
Built on the foundations of a medieval castle, the Louvre served as a
palace for French kings for four hundred years. Recently refurbished,
the Louvre houses one of the world's largest collections of famous art
works including Greco-Roman works like the Venus de Milo and
Winged Victory of Samothrace, and masterpieces of the Italian renaissance like La Giaconda (the Mona Lisa) by Leonardo da Vinci. The
French works include paintings by David, Gericault and Ingres.

Musée d'Orsay: Tel: (0)1 40-49-48-48. Web: www.musee-orsay.fr
Metro Solferino.
Converted from the former Beaux-Arts railway station, the Musée
d'Orsay houses France's largest collection of Impressionist paintings.
The permanent collections include works by Monet, Manet, Degas,
Van Gogh and Cézanne as well as sculpture by Rodin.

Centre Pompidou (Beaubourg). Tel: (0)1 44-78-12-33. Metro Rambuteau.
Built to a controversial design by Richard Rogers and Renzo Piano,
the building with its 'inside out' use of colour coded pipes, electrical
and ventilation ducts attracts even more visitors than the Louvre.
It originally opened in 1977 as a cultural centre embracing music,
cinema, books, graphic arts, etc.

Le Quartier Latin and St. Germain des Prés
One of the oldest 'Arrondissements' of Paris, the Quartier Latin is on
the left bank of the river Seine and gets its name from the students who
have studied the classics there since the 13th century. The Latin
Quarter has cafés, bookshops, and narrow streets with shops and
restaurants.

The Latin Quarter with the next-door St. Germain des Prés became famous in the 1920s for 'La Vie Boheme' – international writers, painters and philosophers frequented the cafés such as Les Deux Magots and Café du Flore, restaurants and bookshops in the narrow streets. The Latin Quarter is home to the University of La Sorbonne and the oldest church in Paris, Eglise de St. Germain des Prés, is close by.

Hôtel des Invalides

This complex of buildings houses museums (including the Musée de l'Armée) and the Eglise St. Louis where Napoleon's funeral took place in 1840 (19 years after his death), and which contains his tomb with the magnificently ornate sarcophagus. A tree-lined esplanade leads to the river, and to the east the Palais Bourbon houses the French parliament.

Montmartre

Built on the side of a steep hill, the Romans, who called this quarter Mons Mars, consecrated an altar to Mercury and a shrine to Mars. When they cut off St. Denis' head in the 3rd century the name was changed to Mont Martyrum (Hill of Martyrs) and then Montmartre. One of the few areas of Paris to remain untouched when the city was redesigned by Baron Hausmann, the steep narrow streets and alleyways of Montmartre became known as the centre of bohemian life. Artists and musicians such as Toulouse-Lautrec, Eric Satie, Modigilani, Utrillo, Apollinaire and Picasso made their homes there. Montmartre abounds with restaurants and cafés and has a reputation for 'risqué' nightlife with such famous nightclubs as Le Moulin Rouge. The hill is crowned by the onion domes and arches of the Basilique du Sacré-Coeur, an enormous white marble Byzantine-cum-Romanesque style structure that was built after the end of the civil war to 'expiate the sins of France'.

Cimitière Père-Lachaise. Tel: (0)1 43-70-70-33. Metro Père Lachaise. The main Paris cemetery has become one of the most visited sites in the city. Along its winding paths, elaborate sarcophagi and head-stones mark the final resting-places of some of the greatest figures in French history. The graves of the writers Balzac, Colette, La Fontaine, Molière and Proust, the painters David and Delacroix, and international figures such as Chopin, Gertrude Stein and Oscar Wilde attract many visitors but the most visited grave is that of the late Jim Morrison, former lead singer with the American rock group The Doors.

LYON:

Lyon is the capital of Rhône Département in southeast central France. Although with a population of 1·5m. it has fewer inhabitants than Marseilles, Lyon is the second largest industrial conurbation after Paris. A leading city in European silk and rayon production, it has many industries, including metal and machine working, and plays a leading role in banking and education. During Roman rule, Julius Caesar used Lyon as a military base to conquer Gaul. Caesar Augustus ordered a network of roads connecting this provincial capital of Gaul with Italy and the Atlantic establishing it as a major crossroads and cultural capital. Lyon remained relatively peaceful through the middle ages. With the introduction of the silk worm from China during the late 15th and early 16th centuries, the silk industry developed and Lyon thrived as a trade centre for northern Europe. Despite a slump in the silk trade during the 18th century and the ravages of the French Revolution, the city prospered again with the introduction of the power loom (a method of weaving invented by Jacquard in 1801). During the 19th century, Lyon was shaken by industrial unrest instigated by the 'Canuts' or silk workers – in one uprising in 1834 hundreds of workers were killed. A century later, during World War II, Lyon served as the centre of the French Resistance movement and was badly bombed just before the city was liberated in Sept. 1944. All but one of the city's bridges was destroyed when the German army retreated. Lyon is the hometown of the Lumière brothers, the inventors of cinema. Today, Lyon is renowned for its industrial success in the production of silk, synthetic fibres, metallurgical and chemical products. Some of the finest chefs in France come from Lyon and the city is justly famous for the excellence of the local cuisine.

TRANSPORT

Airport
Aéroport Lyon-Satolas. Tel: (0)4 72-22-72-21.

The airport was opened in 1975. Flights all over Europe, North Africa, and the Middle East as well as 50 flights daily to Paris. The airport is linked with the city via shuttle buses.

Sato-buses Tel: (0)4 72-22-71-27.

Air France. 10 quai Jules Courmant, 2ème. Tel: (0)8 02-80-28-02.

Air Inter. 100 rue Garibaldi 6ème. Tel: (0)8 02-80-28-02.

Roads
Access by Autoroutes A6, A7, A46, A42 and A 43.

Trains
Lyon has two main-line railway stations.

Perrache and Part-Dieu. Tel: (0)8 36-35-35-35 (reservations and information).

The TGV stops at both stations.

Perrache is more central – located between the Saône and Rhône rivers.

Part-Dieu is in the business district and handles more traffic.

Buses

Long-distance buses run from the Perrache railway station with services to Vienna, Annecy and Grenoble, etc.

Eurolines. Tel: (0)4 72-41-09-09.

Services all over Europe.

Cars Faure. Tel: (0)4 78-96-11-44.

Iberbus. Tel: (0)4 72-41-72-27.

Services to Spain.

Local Transportation

Lyon is served by a Metro system TCL. Tel: (0)4 78-71-80-80.

Maps are available and tickets are sold at TCL offices and tourist offices.

Buses cover the whole city.

Taxis

Taxi Radio de Lyon. Tel: (0)4 72-10-86-86.

TRAVELLERS INFORMATION

Tourist Office. The Pavilion, place Bellecour, 2ème. Metro Bellecour. Tel: (0)4 72-77-69-69.

Email lyoncvb@MicroNet.fr   Web: www.mairie-lyon.fr

Travellers Aid

SOS Voyageurs. Perrache Station. Tel: (0)4 78-37-03-31.

Consulate

UK Consulate. 24 rue Childebert, 2ème. Tel: (0)4 72-77-81-70.
Metro Bellecour.

Financial and Currency

American Express. 6 rue du Childebert, 2ème, Tel: (0)4 72-77-74-50.
Thomas Cook. In Part-Dieu and Perrache railway stations.
Tel: (0)4 72-33-48-55.
Currency exchange also in the tourist offices.
Lyon has over 600 cash ATMs.

Emergency

Medical emergency: Tel: 15
Hospitals. Hôpital Edouard Herriot. 5 place Arsonval.
Tel: (0)4 72-11-73-00.
Hôpital Hôtel Dieu. 1 place de l'Hôpital, 2ème. Tel: (0)4 72-41-30-00.
SOS Médecins. 10 place Dumas de Loire. Tel: (0)4 78-83-51-51.
24-hour home visits.
Other Emergency. Tel: 17
Police. 47 rue de la Charité. Tel: (0)4 78-42-26-56.
Crisis Line.
CISL. Tel: (0)4 78-01-23-45 (foreign visitors).
SOS Amitié. Tel: (0)4 78-29-88-88.

Post Office

Place Antonin Poncet. Tel: (0)4 72-40-65-22.

Internet Access

Connectix Café. 19 quai St. Antoine, 2ème. Tel: (0)4 72-77-98-85.

Landmarks

Cathédrale de St. Jean

Begun at the end of the 12th century, the cathedral was enlarged in the reigns of Philippe Auguste and St Louis. There are 280 remarkable medallions, comparable with those of the chapel in the Papal Palace at Avignon or Rouen cathedral, adorning the west front and depicting sacred, profane and grotesque subjects. The astronomical clock was constructed in the 14th century and on each hour statuettes pop out and ring their bells. Henri IV married Marie de Medici here in 1600.

Musée des Beaux-Arts. 20 place des Terreaux. Tel: (0)4 72-10-17-40. Housed in the St Pierre Palace. Collections include works by Spanish and Dutch masters, Italian Renaissance paintings, French paintings, including works by Gericault and Daumier, and impressionist paintings by artists like Rodin and Monet.

A fine collection of sculpture is shown in a charming garden.

Musée Historique de Tissus. 34 rue de la Charité. Tel: (0)4 79-37-15-05. Traces the growth of the textile industry and the weavers' art in Lyon with fine examples of silk, embroidered satins, embroidery, Louis XV lampas and cut velvets from the Empire and Restoration periods. There are particularly fine examples of woven Lyon silks by Philippe Lasalle. The museum also houses the Centre International d'Études des Textiles Anciens.

La Maison des Canuts. 10–12 rue d'Ivry, 4ème. Tel: (0)4 78-28-62-04.

Demonstrations of the Canuts' impressive ancient art of weaving silk.

Vieux Lyon

The Quartier St. Jean (the area around rue St. Jean, rue de Boeuf and rue Juiverie) contains the colourful 'Hôtel Particuliers' – medieval and Renaissance mansions built by the families of Lyon who became rich as a result of the silk trade. The houses have fancy turrets, shady courtyards and delicate and ornate carvings over their doors. The old town has winding streets with lively cafés and tree-lined squares. The Tourist Office has a list of the Hôtel Particuliers which are open to the public.

Les Traboules

During the height of the silk trade, these long tunnels criss-crossed Vieux Lyon through a maze of courtyards and covered passageways with statuary niches and were constructed to ensure that the silk was safely transported from loom to the storeroom without exposing the delicate silk sheets to the weather. During World War II they provided the French Resistance with routes for spreading intelligence information without detection and as escape routes. The Tourist Office has a list of those Traboules open to the public.

Musée d'Art Contemporain

Cité International de Lyon, quai Charles de Gaulle, 6ème.

Tel: (0)4 72-69-17-18.

This extensive and eclectic collection of modern art is housed in part of a superb modern complex of buildings, which also contain shops, theatres and the international headquarters of Interpol.

Parc de la Tête d'Or

Tel: (0)4 78-89-02-03.

Legend has it that a golden sculpture of the head of Jesus is buried here, hence the name. The park covers over 259 acres and contains a zoo and a botanical garden with two giant greenhouses and rose gardens. Paddleboats are for rent on a huge artificial lake.

Institut Lumière. 25 rue du Premier-Film, 8ème. Tel: (0)4 78-78-18-95. Metro Monplaisir/Lumière.

The museum illustrates the lives of the Lumière brothers who invented the first film projector in 1895. In summer, free films are shown outside the institute each Tuesday.

MARSEILLES:

Marseilles is France's second city, a major seaport and an important industrial centre producing many food products. It is the capital of Bouches-du-Rhône department in southeast France and France's oldest town, settled in the fifth century BC by Greeks and annexed by Rome in 49 BC. During the 11th–14th centuries, it was a commercial centre and transit port for the Holy Land. Taken by Charles I of Anjou (13th century), it was absorbed into and bequeathed to the French crown in 1481. In 1494, Queen Isabella I of Spain declared Marseilles to be the centre of the world and from then the city grew in importance as a gateway to and from the north and sub-Saharan Africa. It grew as a port in the 19th century, with the opening of and the conquest of Algeria. Marseilles to this day remains a multi-national city. It is known for its great avenue, the Canebière, and for the Chateau d'If (1524), a castle in its harbour.

TRANSPORT

Airport

Aéroport Marseille-Provence. Tel: (0)4 42-14-14-14.

Flights to and from Paris, Corsica, Lyon etc. Connects via shuttle bus with the railway station, Gare St. Charles.

Roads

Access by Autoroutes A7, A52 and A57.

Trains

Gare St.Charles, Place Victor Hugo. Tel: (0)8 36-35-35-35.

Trains to and from Paris and Lyon (and local).

Buses

Gare des Autocars. Place Victor Hugo. Tel: (0)4 91-08-16-40.

Long distance buses are run by Car Treize. Tel: (0)4 91-08-16-40 (Car#13) with services to Cassis, Aix-en-Provence, Avignon, Cannes, Nice and Arles.

Local Buses and Metro are run by RTM, 6–8 rue des Farbres. Tel: (0)4 91-91-92-10.

Tickets are sold at metro and bus stops and are valid for both.

Ferries

Run by SNCM. 61 boulevard des Dames. Tel: (0)8 36-67-95-00.

Services to Sardinia and North Africa.

Taxis

Taxi Plus. Tel: (0)4 91-09-28-79.

Marseille Taxi. Tel: (0)4 91-02-20-20.

TRAVELLERS INFORMATION

Tourist Office. 4 rue La Canabière. Tel: (0)4 91-13-89-00.

Web: www.mairie-marseilles.fr

General tourist assistance, free maps and accommodation service.

Consulates

UK Consulate. 24 avenue du Prado. Tel: (0)4 91-15-72-10.

US Consulate. Tel: 12 boulevard Paul Peytral. Tel: (0)4 91-54-92-00.

Financial and Currency

American Express. 39 rue La Canabière. Tel: (0)4 91-13-71-21.

Currency exchange and travel services

Emergency

Emergency: Tel: 17.

Medical Emergency (ambulance). Tel: 15.

Medical Emergency (Home Visit). Tel: (0)4 91-52-84-85.

SOS Médecins (Doctors on call). Tel: (0)4 91-52-91-52.

Pharmacy (late night), check at Tourist Office for rotating list.

Hospital: Hôpital Timone. Boulevard Jean Moulin.

Tel: (0)4 91-38-60-00.

Police. 2 rue du Commissaire Becker. Tel: (0)4 91-16-29-50.

Post Office

1 place Hôtel des Postes. Tel: (0)4 91-15-47-20.

Internet Access

Le Rezo. 68 Cours Julien. Tel: (0)4 91-42-70-02.

L'Internet Café. 25 rue du Village. Tel: (0)4 91-42-09-37.

Car Hire

See central reservation numbers on page 156.

Hotel Reservations

See central reservation numbers on page 155.

Landmarks

Abbaye St. Victor. rue Saint and quai de Rive Neuve.

Tel: (0)4 91-33-25-86.

St Victor is believed to have met a martyr's death on this spot at the beginning of the 4th century and the abbey was supposed to have been built in his memory. It was rebuilt in 1040 and the crypt was altered in the Gothic period. The 5th century catacombs and basilica contain an impressive array of pagan and Christian relics and the 4th century sarcophagi are justly famous.

Basilique de Notre Dame de la Garde. Tel: (0)4 91-13-40-80.
Situated above the city, the church itself is 19th century but offers
unparalleled views of the harbour islands, Château d'If and the
surrounding mountains.

Château d'If. Tel: (0)4 91-59-02-30.
It is a short boat ride to the Ile d'If (one of Marseilles' harbour islands)
on which is located the Chateau harbouring the infamous dungeons
immortalized in Alexandre Dumas' *The Count of Monte Cristo* and
The Man in the Iron Mask.

Musée des Beaux-Arts. boulevard Long Champ. Tel: (0)4 91-14-59-30.
The museum houses a collection of French painting from the 16th to
the 19th centuries and 17th to 19th century sculpture. There is also an
interesting collection of provençal paintings. Artists include Corbet
and Rubens and there are 36 political satire busts by Daumier. The
building itself is one of Marseilles' prettiest sights.

Musée d'Histoire Naturelle. Tel: (0)4 91 62 30 78.
As well as the museum, there is an aquarium with living examples of
regional marine life. Behind the museum is the Jardin Zoologique.

LILLE:

Lille is the capital of Nord department in northern France. Founded in
the 11th century, Lille was established as an island transit town for
boats passing down the river Deûle. Once chief city of the county of
Flanders and home of the 16th-century Dukes of Burgundy, Lille was
captured by the Duke of Marlborough in 1708 and restored to France
by the Treaty of Utrecht in 1713. Lille was Charles de Gaulle's hometown and has retained much of its Flemish favour, particularly in the

food and drink to be found here. Long known for its textiles, Lille is today at the heart of a large, industrially developed metropolitan area although one quarter of the population are students and this gives the town a bustling atmosphere and a varied nightlife.

TRANSPORT

Airport

Lille airport is 8 km from the city centre.

Roads

Access by Autoroutes A1, A22, A23, A25, and A27.

Trains

Lille has two railway stations:

Gare Lille Flandres. Tel (0)8 36-35-35-35. Trains to and from Paris, Arras and Brussels.

Gare Lille Europe. Tel: (0)3 20-87-30-00. Services Eurostar (London or Brussels) and all TGV trains to the south of France.

Lille has a Metro, tramway and bus service.

Buses

The central bus terminal is next to the Gare Lille Flandres.

Central taxi service: (0)3 20-06-06-06.

Car Hire

See central reservation numbers on page 156.

Bicycle Hire

Peugeot Cycles. 64 rue Léon Gambetta. Tel: (0)3 20-54-83-39.

TRAVELLERS INFORMATION

SOS Voyageurs. On platform (voie) 9, Gare de Lille Flandres.
Tel: (0)3 20-31-62-12.
  Tourist Office. place Rihour. Tel: (0)3 20-21-94-21.
Web: www.mairie-lille.fr
  Free accommodation service, maps and mass transit guide. Also offers currency exchange.

Financial and Currency
24-hour ATMs are available on the place de la République.

Emergency
Medical emergency: Tel 15.
Hospital. 2 avenue Oscar Lambret. Tel: (0)3 20-44-59-62.
Other emergency: Tel: 17.

Police: 10 rue Ovigneur. Tel: (0)3 20-57-41-22.

Crisis Line: Nul à la vie. Tel: (0)8 00-23-52-36.

Post Office
8 place de la République. Tel: (0)3 20-12-74-72.

Internet Access
NetPlayer Games. 25 boulevard Carnot. Tel: (0)3 20-31-20-29.

Hotel Reservations
See central reservation numbers on page 155.

Car Hire
See central reservation numbers on page 156.

Landmarks

Musée de l'Art Moderne. 1 allée du Musée. Tel: (0)3 20-19-68-68. Houses an impressive collection of works by cubists and post-modern artists including Picasso, Braque, Léger, Miro and Modigliani.

Musée des Beaux-Arts. place de la Republique. Tel: (0)3 20-06-78-00. Houses a large collection of mid-19th century French paintings.

La Vieille Bourse. place du General de Gaulle.
A masterpiece of Flemish architecture. The four buildings surround a courtyard that once housed the old Stock Exchange and now house flower and book markets.

Vieux Lille. (The old town)
The medieval streets of the old town of Lille have many houses and shops embellished with swags, masks and carved pilasters, and small traditional cafés and restaurants.

La Citadelle
A pentagonal fortress rebuilt in the 17th century to designs by Vauban surrounded by a canal and gardens.

Birthplace of Charles de Gaulle. 9 rue Princess. Tel: (0)3 20-31-96-03. Houses a large collection of photographs and press clippings, his car and christening robe.

Local Festivals

In the last week in April Lille hosts three festivals.
Journées des Villes Fortifiées. Tel: (0)3 20-52-47-23.
Festival du Film Court and Festival de Lille (which highlights differing world cultures).

BORDEAUX:

Situated on the Garonne River, Bordeaux is the capital of the Gironde department in southwest France. It is a busy port, accessible to the Atlantic, with important shipyards and industries. The region is known for producing fine wines. A prosperous Roman city, it flourished during the 11th century as the seat of the dukes of Acquitaine. Eleanor of Acquitaine's first marriage to the future King Louis VII was annulled after 15 years and her dowry, which had included Bordeaux as well as most of southwestern France, was returned to her. Her subsequent marriage to Henry Plantagenet allied the city with England and from 1360 Bordeaux served as a base for the Black Prince during his campaigns against French-held possessions in the southwest. In 1453 the Battle of Castillon put the town under French rule again. The English demand for wine was the main factor in the expansion of the port of Bordeaux and the merchants of Bordeaux grew rich exporting and developing the great wines of the region from the châteaux along the banks of the Garonne and Dordogne rivers, tributaries of the Gironde. The French revolution saw a feud between a group of Bordeaux 'deputés' known as the Girondins, who were persecuted by another faction (the Montagnards) for conspiring against the revolution. Twenty-three of them were rounded up and executed.

The city reached its height of prosperity in the 18th century when the 'Intendents' (high-ranking representatives of the French crown) transformed the medieval city into their vision of a well-planned city with wide boulevards, quayside avenues and classical buildings like the Hôtel de Ville and the Grand Théâtre.

Bordeaux was the temporary seat of the French government in 1914 and 1940 (during World Wars I and II). Modern Bordeaux has a population of 700,000 and, apart from businesses connected with the wine trade, supports a major university, research facilities and some aerospace industries. The local government has undertaken a major programme of restoration of the cathedral, mansions and historic monuments. As well as being renowned for some of the best food in France, Bordeaux remains a centre for wine connoisseurs. According to Henry James, the city is 'dedicated to the worship of Bacchus in the most discreet form'.

TRANSPORT

Airport
Airport at Mérignac. Tel: (0)5 56-34-50-00.
Air France. Tel: (0)5 56-00-40-40.
Air Inter. Tel: (0)5 56-13-10-10.
   The airport is linked with Bordeaux by a shuttle bus to the train station and tourist office.

Roads
Access by autoroutes A10, A62, A63.

Trains
Gare St. Jean. rue Charles Domerq. Tel: (0)5 56-92-50-50.
   TGV to Paris and trains to other long-distance French destinations.

Buses
Eurolines. rue Charles Domerq. Tel: (0)5 56-92-50-42.
Web: www.eurolines.fr
Long distance to Spain, etc.
Trans-Gironde. Allées de Bristol. Tel: (0)5 56-99-33-33.
Local bus service to Arcachon, Biscarosse and Mimizan.

Local Transportation
CGTFE, 4 rue Georges Bonnac. Tel: (0)5 57-57-88-88.

City buses run by CGFTE cover the city. 1- or 3-day passes (Carte Bordeaux Découverte) available.

Taxis

Aquitaine Taxi radio. Tel: (0)5 56-86-80-31.

Bicycle Hire

Cycles Pasteur. 42 cours Pasteur. Tel: (0)5 56-92-68-20.
Or at the Tourist Office (see below)

TRAVELLERS INFORMATION

Tourist Office

12 cours du 30 Juillet. Tel: (0)5 56-00-66-00.
Web: www.bordeaux-tourism.com
email: otb@bordeaux-tourisme.com
Branch at the Gare St. Jean.

Consulate

UK Consulate. 353 boulevard du President Wilson (0)5 57-22-21-10.
emergency (0)5 57-22-01-43.

Financial and Currency

Thomas Cook. Gare St. Jean, rue Charles Domerq.
Tel: (0)5 56-91-58-80.
American Express. 14 cours de l'Intendance.
Tel: (0)5 56-00-63-33; refund 0 800 90 86 00.
Currency exchange also at the Tourist Office and Post Office.
Cash ATMs all over the city.
Credit Mutuel. 61 cours de l'Intendance and other locations.

Emergency

Medical Emergency: Tel: 15.

Other Emergency. Tel: 17.

Hospital. 1 rue Jean Burguet. Tel: (0)5 56-79-56-79.

Crisis Line. SOS Amitié. Tel: (0)5 56-44-22-22.

Police. 87 rue de l'Abbé de l'Epée (AKA rue Castéja).

Tel: (0)5 56-99-77-77.

Internet Access

L'Héroique Sandwich. 47 rue St. James. Tel: (0)5 56-52-76-63.

Cyberstation. 23 cours Pasteur. Tel: (0)5 56-01-15-15.

Car Hire

See central reservation numbers on page 156.

Hotel Reservations

See central reservation numbers on page 155.

Landmarks

Grand Théâtre. (Opera de Bordeaux). place de la Comédie.
Tel: (0)5 56-48-58-54.

Recently restored, this is one of the finest theatres in France. It was built in 1773–1802 in the classical style by Victor Louis. The exterior has a magnificent colonnade running all around the building with 12 huge statues of muses and goddesses surmounting the front façade. The interior great staircase (which was later copied by Garnier for l'Opéra in Paris) is considered a triumph and the auditorium with its cantilevered boxes, carved pillars and ramps was designed with acoustics in mind.

Cathédrale St. André. place Pey-Berland. Tel: (0)5 56-52-68-10.
Originally consecrated by Pope Urban II, this gothic masterpiece was

built between the 11th and 16th centuries but after two hundred years
of neglect, it was extensively renovated in the 19th century.

Tour Pey-Berland. place Pey-Berland.
Built as the bell tower for the cathedral, this Italian style 'campanile'
rises 63 metres into the sky and offers panoramic views across the city.

Monument des Girondins. esplanade des Quinconces.
The 50 metre high Statue of Liberty casting off her chains with bronze
fountains on either side (named Le Triomphe de la République and
Le Triomphe de la Concorde) commemorates the Girondins who
perished in the French Revolution.

Quartier des Chartons
The old town of Bordeaux is located behind the quayside and was
devoted to the wine trade and ships' chandlers. It became fashionable in the 18th century when the city's rich families built great
houses. The streets are lined with houses with classical façades and
wrought-iron balconies.

Musée des Beaux-Arts. 20 cours d'Albert. Tel: (0)5 56-10-17-18.
Originally created by Napoleon to house war booty, spacious galleries
now contain paintings by Titan, Delacroix, Renoir, Matisse and others.
There is also an impressive collection of 17th century French, Italian
and Dutch paintings and several rooms of contemporary paintings.

Musée d'Aquitaine. 20 cours Pasteur. Tel: (0)5 51-01-51-02.
There are several important archaeological and antique works, and a
comprehensive exhibition of local history and ethnography which
illustrates the growth of the port and the history of the wine industry.

Maison du Vin/CIVB. 1 cours du 30 Juillet. Tel: (0)5 56-00-22-66/
(0)5 50-00-22-88.
The wine information centre for the region offers opportunities to taste –
sometimes free. There is a 2-hour 'Initiation to Wine Tasting' and the

Centre can arrange for tours of the local wine-producing 'Châteaux' (in this context, Château means the headquarters of a vineyard, not 'castle').

TOULOUSE:

Toulouse is the capital of Haute-Garonne department and lies on the Garonne River. A cultural and commercial centre, Toulouse is the sixth largest city in France and the centre of the French aerospace industry. Toulouse is linked by the river Garonne to the Atlantic, by the Lauraguais pass to the Mediterranean and by the valleys through the Pyrenees to Spain and has, over the centuries, been open to many influences. As part of Roman Gaul, it was (419–508) the capital of the Visigoths and between the 9th and 13th centuries, Toulouse enjoyed great prosperity. By the start of the 13th century, the people of Haute-Languedoc were repelled by the corruption of the Catholic church and were increasingly drawn to the Cathar religion – a heretical belief based on Christian scriptures but preaching an ascetic lifestyle. The Pope, bent on rooting out this heresy, excommunicated the Count of Toulouse and launched a crusade against the Cathars. They took refuge in Albi (becoming known thereafter as 'Albigensians') and in the neighbouring châteaux of sympathetic nobles; but the catholic troops, backed by King Philippe-Auguste of France, searched them out and in 1244, 200 Cathars were burned alive at the Château de Ségur. The end of the Albigensian Crusade brought Toulouse back under French rule. After the turmoil of the Albigensian crisis, Toulouse became, once more, the artistic and literary centre of medieval Europe. An academy was founded and literary societies blossomed. The discovery of 'pastel', a plant that produced a pale blue dye that became extremely popular all over Europe, added to the prosperity of the region. In the 18th century, thermal springs proved popular with the prosperous French wanting to take the waters.

Toulouse is now the centre of the French aerospace industry, having had a long history of pioneering aviation. Toulouse can claim credit for several important breakthroughs in military aviation – and for the development of many civil aircraft, among them the Caravelle and Concorde, which were developed in co-operation with Germany and Britain. Satellites are launched from Ariane rockets and the Airbus has become one of the most popular civil aircraft ever produced.

TRANSPORT

Airport
Aéroport Blagnac. 10 km west of Toulouse. Tel: (0)5 61-42-44-00.
European flights.
Air Liberté. Tel: (0)8 03-80-58-05.
12 flights daily to Paris.
Air France. 2 boulevard de Strasbourg. Tel: (0)8 02-80-28-02.
25 flights to Paris and flights to other European destinations.

The airport is connected to Toulouse centre by bus.
Navettes Aérocar. Tel: (0)5 61-30-04-89 and (0)5 61-16-49-00.
Runs buses to and from Aéroport Blagnac and Allées Jaurès in Toulouse centre.

Roads
Access by Autoroutes A10, A61, A62, A63, A64, A66 and A68.

Trains
Gare Matabiau. boulevard Pierre Sémard. Tel: (0)8 36 35 35 35.
Trains to Paris, Bordeaux, Perpignan, Lyon, etc.

Tickets can be bought at the station or at Espace Transport. 7 place Esquirol. Tel: (0)5 61-41-70-70.

Buses

Gare Routière. 68–70 boulevard Pierre Sémard. Tel: (0)5 61-61-67-67. Long distance routes.

Toulouse has a comprehensive bus service run by:
SEMVAT. 7 place Esquirol. Tel: (0)5 61-41-70-70 or (0)5 62-11-26-11. Buy tickets on the bus or at ticket booths.

Taxis

Taxi Bleue. Tel: (0)5 61-80-36-36.

TRAVELLERS INFORMATION

Tourist Office. Donjon du Câpitol, rue Lafayette, sq. Charles de Gaulle. Tel: (0)5 61-11-02-22.
Web: www.mairie-toulouse.fr   Email: Ottoulouse@mipnet.fr

Travellers Aid

SOS Voyageurs. Gare Matabiau. boulevard Pierre Sémard. Tel: (0)5 61-62-27-30.

Financial and Currency

American Express. 73 rue d'Alsace-Lorraine. Tel: (0)5 61-21-78-25. Banque de France. 4 rue Deville. Tel: (0)5 61-61-35-35.

Emergency

Medical emergency: 15.
Other emergency: 17.

Hospital. CHR de Rangueil, Chemin de Vallon. Tel: (0)5 62-30-25-33.

Ambulance. Tel: (0)5 61-31-56-00.

Police. Commissariat Central. Tel: (0)5 61-12-77-77.

Crisis Line. SOS Amitié. Tel: (0)5 61-80-80-80.

Post Office

9 rue de Lafayette. Tel: (0)5 62-15-30-00.

Internet Access

Cybercopie. 18 rue des Lois and 5 place de Deyrou.

Tel: (0)5 61-21-03-71.

Icon. 14 rue Bachelier. Tel: (0)5 62-73-71-81.

Hotel Reservations

See listings for central reservations on page 155.

Car Hire

See listings for central reservations on page 156.

Landmarks

Basilique St. Sernin

This is now (after the destruction of Cluny) the largest Romanesque
building in France and contains the greatest number of holy relics.
The original basilica held the body of St. Sernin (or Saturnius), the first
bishop of Toulouse, who was martyred in 250 by being tied to the tail
(some say legs) of the bull he refused to sacrifice to pagan gods.
Charlemagne later donated so many relics that the church became
the focus of many European pilgrims on their way to Santiago de
Compostela across the border in Spain. The present building was
constructed between the 11th and 14th centuries and, although
remaining relatively untouched, the church's exterior was renovated
under Violet le Duc in the 19th century.

Eglise Notre Dame du Taur. 12 rue du Taur. Tel: (0)5 61-21-41-57. This church marks the spot where St Sernin's (Saturnius) ride on the bull's tail ended in his death. The enormous fresco over the altar commemorates the event.

Musée des Augustins. 21 rue de Metz (off rue Alsace-Lorraine). Tel: (0)5 61-22-21-82. Housed in a former Augustinian monastery designed in the southern French gothic style and built during the 14th and 15th centuries. The buildings house collections of Romanesque and Gothic sculptures, paleo-Christian archaeological artefacts and works of art from the 15th, 16th and 17th centuries.

Les Jacobins. (and Réfectoire des Jacobins) 69 rue Pargaminières. Tel: (0)5 61-22-21-92. An excellent example of 'Gothique du Midi' or southern gothic style, this monastery was founded in 1215 by St. Dominique as a refuge against the Albigensian heresy. It served as the first university in Toulouse. St Thomas Aquinas is buried in the main church. The 'Réfectoire' acts as a space for various exhibitions.

Hôtel d'Assézat. place d'Assézat. Tel: (0)5 61-12-06-89. The finest private mansion in Toulouse, it was built in the mid-15th century for Capitoul d'Assézat who had made a fortune trading in dyer's woad. It was donated to the learned societies of Toulouse in 1896 and now houses the magnificent collection of Georges Bemberg. Italian masterpieces include works by Canaletto, Guardi, Tiepolo, Tintoretto and Veronese. Flemish and Dutch masters include Van der Weyden and Cranach the Elder. The collections of French painting include works by Bonnard, Matisse, Dufy, Braque, Monet, Sisley, Caillebotte and Boudin.

Tour of the Old City. Information from the tourist office. Tel: (0)5 61-11-02-22.

This 2-hour walking tour takes in the stone mansion or 'Hotels Particuliers' built by the rich families of Toulouse in the 15th and 16th centuries.

La Cité de l'Espace. Parc de la Plaine, avenue Jean Gonord.
Tel: (0)5 62-71-64-80.
A new park devoted to Toulouse's space programmes.

LANGUAGES

The official language is French. Breton and Basque are spoken in their regions. The *Toubon* legislation of 1994 seeks to restrict the use of foreign words in official communications, broadcasting and advertisements (a previous such decree dated from 1975). The Constitutional Court has since ruled that imposing such restrictions on private citizens would infringe their freedom of expression.
Monnier, A., *La Population de la France.* Paris, 1990

SOCIAL STATISTICS

Statistics for calendar years:

	Marriages	Births	Deaths
1995	254,000	727,800	532,000
1996	279,000	734,000	536,000

Live birth rate (1996) was 12·6 per 1,000 population; death rate, 9·2; marriage rate, 4·8. Divorces, 1995, 117,000; rate, 2·0 per 1,000 population. 38% of births in 1995 were outside marriage. In 1994 the most popular age range for marrying was 25–29 for both males and females. Abortions were legalized in 1975; there were 162,620 in 1990. Life expectancy at birth, 1990–95, 73·8 years for males and 82·4 years for females. Annual growth rate, 1990–95, 0·5%. From 1990–95 the suicide rate per 100,000 population was 20·1 (men, 29·6; women, 11·1). Infant mortality, 1990–95, 7 per 1,000 live births; fertility rate, 1·7 births per woman.

CLIMATE

The north-west has a moderate maritime climate, with small temperature range and abundant rainfall; inland, rainfall becomes more seasonal, with a summer maximum, and the annual range of temperature increases. Southern France has a Mediterranean climate, with mild moist winters and hot dry summers. Eastern France has a continental climate and a rainfall maximum in summer, with thunderstorms prevalent. Paris, Jan. 37°F (3°C), July 64°F (18°C). Annual rainfall 22·9" (573 mm). Bordeaux, Jan. 41°F (5°C), July 68°F (20°C). Annual rainfall 31·4" (786 mm). Lyons, Jan. 37°F (3°C), July 68°F (20°C). Annual rainfall 31·8" (794 mm).

CONSTITUTION AND GOVERNMENT

France has a highly centralized system of government which assumes a close relationship between citizens and the state. Every French village has an imposing town hall, identified by a tricolor flag and every département has a grand préfecture as home to the unelected representative from Paris. The French state spends around 54% of GDP, one of the highest proportions in Europe, and employs one in four workers. Most leading politicians are former civil servants.

The Constitution of the Fifth Republic, superseding that of 1946, came into force on 4 Oct. 1958. It consists of a preamble, dealing with the Rights of Man, and 92 articles.

France is a republic, indivisible, secular, democratic and social; all citizens are equal before the law (Art. 1). National sovereignty resides with the people, who exercise it through their representatives and by referendums (Art. 3). Constitutional reforms of July 1995 widened the range of issues on which referendums may be called. Political parties carry out their activities freely, but must respect the principles of national sovereignty and democracy (Art. 4).

A constitutional amendment of 4 Aug. 1995 deleted all references to the 'community' (*communauté*) between France and her overseas possessions, representing an important step towards the constitutional dismantling of the former French colonial empire.

The head of state is the President, who sees that the Constitution is respected; ensures the regular functioning of the public authorities, as well as the continuity of the state; is the protector of national independence and territorial integrity (Art. 5). The President is elected for 7 years by direct universal suffrage (Art. 6). The President appoints (and dismisses) a Prime Minister and, on the latter's advice, appoints and dismisses the other members of the Government (*Council of Ministers*) (Art. 8); presides over the Council of Ministers (Art. 9); may dissolve the National Assembly, after consultation with the Prime Minister and the Presidents of the two Houses (Art. 12); appoints to the civil and military offices of the state (Art. 13). In times of crisis, the President may take such emergency powers as the circumstances demand; the National Assembly cannot be dissolved during such a period (Art. 16).

Parliament consists of the National Assembly and the Senate. The National Assembly is elected by direct suffrage by the second ballot system (by which candidates winning 50% or more of the vote in their constituencies are elected, candidates winning less than 12·5% are eliminated and other candidates go on to a second round of voting); the Senate is elected by indirect suffrage (Art. 24). Since 1996 the National Assembly has convened for an annual 9-month session. It comprises 577 deputies, elected by a two-ballot system for a 5-year term from single-member constituencies (555 in Metropolitan France, 22 in the overseas departments and dependencies); and may be dissolved by the President.

The *Senate* comprises 321 senators elected for 9-year terms (one-third every 3 years) by an electoral college in each Department or overseas dependency, made up of all members of the Departmental Council or its equivalent in overseas dependencies, together with all members of Municipal Councils within that area. The *Speaker* of the Senate deputizes for the President of the Republic in the event of the latter's incapacity. Senate elections were last held on 27 Sept. 1998.

The *Constitutional Council* is composed of 9 members whose term of office is 9 years (non-renewable), one-third every 3 years; 3 are appointed by the President of the Republic, 3 by the President of the National Assembly, 3 by the President of the Senate; in addition, former Presidents of the Republic are, by right, life members of the Constitutional Council (Art. 56). It oversees the fairness of the elections of the President (Art. 58) and Parliament (Art. 59), and of referendums (Art. 60), and acts as a guardian of the Constitution (Art. 61). Its *President* is Roland Dumas (app. 1995).

The *Economic and Social Council* advises on Government and Private Members' Bills (Art. 69). It comprises representatives of employers', workers' and farmers' organizations in each Department and Overseas Territory.

Ameller, M., *L'Assemblée Nationale.* Paris, 1994

Duhamel, O. and Mény, Y., *Dictionnaire Constitutionnel.* Paris, 1992

Elgie, R. (ed.) *Electing the French President: the 1995 Presidential Election.* Macmillan, London, 1996

National Anthem.

'La Marseillaise'; words and tune by C. Rouget de Lisle.

RECENT ELECTIONS

At the first round of presidential elections on 23 April 1995, Lionel Jospin gained the largest number of votes (23·31% of those cast) against 8 opponents. At the second round on 7 May 1995, the electorate was 39,976,944; turn-out was 79·77%. Jacques Chirac was elected President against Jospin by 52·64% of votes cast.

At the elections of 25 May and 1 June 1997 to the National Assembly, there were 6,361 candidates; the electorate was 38,968,660. In the first round, turn-out was 68·93%. The Socialist Party (PS) and allies won 253 seats; the Rassemblement pour la République (RPR; Gaullists), 134; the Union for French Democracy (UDF), 108; the Communist Party (PCF), 38; Greens, 7; other left parties, 21; other right parties, 15; National Front, 1.

Following the election held on 27 Sept. 1998, the Senate was composed of (by group, including affiliates): RPR, 99; PS, 78; Union Centriste (UC), 52; Républicains et Indépendants (RI), 47; Rassemblement Démocratique et Europeén Social (RDES), 22; Républicain, Communiste et Citoyen (RCC), 16; Unattached, 7. In Oct. 1998 Christian Poncelet (RPR) was elected *Speaker* for a 3-year term.

European Parliament. France has 87 representatives. At the June 1999 elections turn-out was 47·0%. The PS won 22 seats with 22·0% of votes cast (political affiliation in European Parliament: European Socialist Party); RPFIE (Euro Sceptics RPF), 13 with 13·0% (Group of Independents for a Europe of Nations); the RPR-DL (Gaullists), 12 with 12·8% (European People's Party); the Greens, 9 with 9·7%

(Greens); UDF, 9 with 9·3% (European People's Party). Other parties gained 6 seats or fewer.

CURRENT ADMINISTRATION

President: Jacques Chirac (RPR; sworn in 17 May 1995).

A new left-wing coalition government (including the anti-Euro Communist group) was formed on 4 June 1997, consisting in Sept. 1999 of:

Prime Minister: Lionel Jospin (PS); *Minister of Justice and Keeper of the Seals:* Elisabeth Guigou (PS). *Foreign Affairs:* Hubert Védrine (PS). *Interior:* Jean-Pierre Chevènement (MDC). *Economy, Finance and Industry:* Dominique Strauss-Kahn (PS). *Defence:* Alain Richard (PS). *Employment and Solidarity:* Martine Aubry (PS). *Education, Research and Technology:* Claude Allègre (PS). *Public Works, Transport and Housing:* Jean-Claude Gayssot (PC). *Relations with the Parliament:* Daniel Vaillant (PS). *Environment and Regional Development:* Dominique Voynet (Green). *Culture and Communication, and Government Spokeswoman:* Catherine Trautmann (PS). *Agriculture, Fisheries and Food:* Jean Glavany (PS). *Civil Service, Administrative Reform and Decentralization:* Emile Zuccarelli (PRS). *Youth and Sport:* Marie-Georges Buffet (PC).

Ministers-Delegate include*: European Affairs:* Pierre Moscovici (PS). *Foreign Trade:* François Huwart (Greens). *Overseas Territories:* Jean-Jack Queyranne (PS). *Industry:* Christian Pierret (PS). *Tourism:* Michelle Demessine (PC). *Housing:* Louis Besson (PS). *Education:* Ségolène Royal (PS). *Health and Social Action:* Dominique Gillot (PS). *Budget:* Christian Sautter. *Veterans and War Victims:* Jean-Pierre Masseret (PS). *Co-operation:* Charles Josselin. *Small and Medium Business, Commerce and Craft:* Marylise Lebranchu.

POLITICAL AND FINANCIAL PROFILES

President of the Republic

Jacques Chirac

Jacques Chirac was born on 29 Nov. 1932. He graduated from the Institut d'Études Politiques de Paris in 1954, served as an army officer in Algeria (1956–57), and earned a graduate degree from the École Nationale d'Administration in 1959. He then became a civil servant and rose rapidly through the ranks, serving as a department head and a Secretary of State before becoming Minister for Parliamentary Relations in 1971–72 under President Georges Pompidou. Chirac was elected to the National Assembly as a Gaullist successively from 1967. After serving as Minister of Agriculture (1972–74) and the Interior (1974), Chirac was appointed Prime Minister by the newly elected President Giscard. After Chirac resigned from that office in 1976, he was elected Mayor of Paris the next year. He proceeded to build up a powerful political base by appealing to radical conservative interests. It was on his third attempt that Mayor Jacques Chirac of Paris at last succeeded to the French presidency. In May 1995, Chirac won against the Socialist Party (PS) candidate, Lionel Jospin, now Prime Minister. With France facing a soaring budget deficit and steadily rising unemployment, Chirac convinced voters that a change was needed.

Prime Minister

Lionel Jospin

Lionel Jospin was born in the Parisian suburb of Meudon in 1937. After two years of obligatory military service, he entered the École Nationale d'Administration in 1963 and after graduating near the top of his class, he joined the Foreign Ministry. In the late 1960s, Jospin went to the USA to study. In 1970 he returned to France and took a position at the University Institute of Technology of Paris-Sceaux, where he taught economics until 1981. Jospin joined the Socialist Party (PS) in 1971 and won his first parliamentary seat six years later. He soon became a favourite of party leader François Mitterrand and when Mitterrand became president in 1981, Jospin was promoted to head the party. He became minister of education during Mitterrand's second term.

Jospin lost his Cabinet post in 1992 and his parliamentary seat in 1993. In 1995, with Mitterrand dying and the party under threat from revelations of financial improprieties, the party turned to Jospin as its candidate for president. Although Jospin won the first round, he ultimately lost to Jacques Chirac. When scandal again haunted the PS leaders in 1997, Jospin was asked to be the party's candidate for Prime Minister. He was elected Prime Minister on 4 June 1997.

Minister of Foreign Affairs
Hubert Védrine

Hubert Védrine was born in 1947 and was educated in Paris at the Institut d'Études Politiques and the École Nationale d'Administration. From 1974 to 1978 Védrine served as a senior civil servant at the Ministry of Culture, acting as head of the office responsible for town conservation. In 1978 he was appointed head of the Conservation and Enhancement of the Architectural Site division at the Ministry of Culture and then at the Ministry for Capital Works. From 1979 to 1981 he was attached to the Director-General of the Ministry of Foreign Affairs' Cultural, Scientific and Technical Directorate and in 1981 he became diplomatic advisor to the President of the Republic. From 1988 to 1991 he acted as spokesman for the Presidency of the Republic and in 1991 for the Secretary-General of the Presidency of the Republic. He served the Conseils d'États in 1995–1996 and also led a seminar on Decision-Making in Foreign Policy at the École des Hautes Études en Sciences Sociale.

Hubert Védrine is the author of *'Les Mondes de François Mitterrand à l'Elysée'*, 1981–1995 (Fayard, 1996) and he was a partner in the law firm of Jeantet et Associés from 1996 until May 1997.

Minister of Defence

Alain Richard

Alain Richard was born and brought up in Paris. He took a degree in Law and in 1962 joined the Parti Socialiste Unifié. After doing his military service, Richard taught simultaneously at Reims and Paris Universities, serving as a member of the PSU national Bureau from 1972–74. In 1975 he joined the Parti Socialiste (PS) becoming the PS National Assembly Deputy for Val d'Oise from 1978–93 and during this period he also served as Secretary and then Chairman of the Socialist Group (1978–86). From 1981–86 he led a majority group on the committee responsible for reviewing legislation, playing an active role in the many reforms instituted. Since 1981 Richard has been a member of the PS steering committee and has held various posts in the organization including National Secretary for elections and National Delegate for financial matters. From 1988–93 he was closely associated with the majority party's economic and financial policy in his capacity as General Rapporteur for the Finance Committee. In 1995 he was elected Senator for Val d'Oise and was appointed Secretary of the Senate Finance Committee. Richard is a member of the Senate European Union Delegation and a member of the Local Finance committee.

Governor of the Banque de France (and Inspecteur Général des Finances)

Jean-Claude Trichet

Jean-Claude Trichet was born in Lyon in 1942. He is an Ingénieur Civil des Mines (mining engineer) and Licencié en Science Économiques. He is a graduate of the Institut d'Études Politiques and the École

Nationale d'Administration. M. Trichet was economic adviser to the Minister for Economic Affairs and Finance (René Monory) in 1978 and in the same year, he became Adviser to the President of the Republic (Valéry Giscard d'Estaing) on industry, energy and research. In 1981 he became head of the Office for Development Aid of the Treasury and Director of Bilateral Affairs at the Treasury. Also in 1981 he was head of International Affairs, and Treasury Member of the Board of Compagnie Financière Paribas. In 1986 Trichet became Chief of Staff (Directeur de Cabinet) to the Minister of Economic Affairs, Finance and Privatization (Edouard Balladur) and, a year later, Directeur du Trésor (Under-secretary at the treasury). He was appointed Governor of the Banque de France (France's National Bank) in 1993. Jean-Claude Trichet has served on a number of national and international committees including B.N.P. (board member), Censor of Banque de France, European Monetary Committee (Chairman 1992–93), Paris Club (sovereign debt rescheduling) 1985–93, Member, Board of Governors of the World Bank, Member, Boards of the Bank for International Settlements and the Monetary Institute.

LOCAL GOVERNMENT

France is divided into 22 regions for national development, planning and budgetary policy. Many of these regions are broadly comparable with the provinces of pre-revolutionary France, and give a measure of recognition to the distinctive personalities of peripheral areas such as Alsace and Brittany.

By a law of 13 May 1991 Corsica became a territorial collectivity. After the regional elections of March 1992 it had an assembly which elects an executive council. Since Feb. 1995 the Pays Basque, which formed part of the department Pyrénées-Atlantique, has had

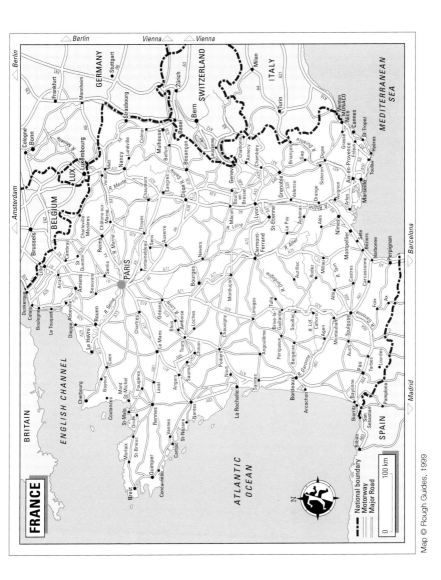

FRANCE

BRITAIN

ENGLISH CHANNEL

ATLANTIC
OCEAN

△ Berlin
△ Berlin

GERMANY

Frankfurt
Mannheim
Stuttgart

Cologne
Bonn

R. Moselle

BELGIUM
Brussels

LUX
Luxembourg

Metz
Nancy
Lunéville
Strasbourg
Colmar
Mulhouse

Vienna △
△ Vienna

Zürich
SWITZERLAND
Bern

Milan
ITALY

Turin

Amsterdam

Lille
Cambrai
Charleville
Mézières
Reims
Chálons-sur-Marne

St Quentin
Arras
Amiens
Beauvais

Dunkerque
Calais
Boulogne
Le Touquet
Dieppe
Abbeville
Le Havre
Rouen

R. Seine

PARIS

Senlis

Troyes
Auxerre

Chaumont
R. Meuse
Verdun
Langres
Dijon
R. Saône

Mácon
Bourg-en-Bresse

Besançon
Lausanne
Geneva
Chamonix
Annecy
Chambéry

Briançon
Gap

Menton
MONACO
Nice
Cannes
St-Tropez
Fréjus
Grasse
Aix-en-Provence
Hyères
Toulon

MEDITERRANEAN
SEA

Fontainebleau
Sens

Nevers

Bourges

R. Loire
Lyon
St-Etienne

Valence
Grenoble

Sisteron
Digne

Orange
Avignon
Arles
Marseille
R. Durance

Chartres
Orléans
Blois
Amboise
Tours
Loches
Chinon
Chauvigny
Poitiers

R. Cher
R. Loire

Montlucon
Clermont-Ferrand
Le Puy
Aubenas
Alès
Nîmes
Montpellier
Sète
Béziers

R. Rhône

Cherbourg
Bayeux
Coutances
Mont
St-Michel
St-Malo
Dinan
St-Brieuc
Fougères

Caen

Laval
Angers
Saumur

Le Mans

Nantes
St-Nazaire
Vannes
Carnac

Rennes

Niort

La Rochelle

Angoulême
Limoges
Brive-la-Gaillarde
Tulle
Souillac
Périgueux
Bergerac
R. Lot
Cahors
R. Dordogne
Aurillac
Rodez
Millau
R. Tarn
Castres
Albi
Carcassonne
Narbonne
Perpignan
R. Aude
Foix

Bordeaux
Arcachon
Bayonne
Biarritz
Bilbao
San
Sebastián
Pamplona
SPAIN

Agen
Montauban
Toulouse
Auch
Pau
Tarbes
Lourdes
R. Garonne

Morlaix
Quimper
Concarneau
Brest

△ Barcelona
△ Madrid

N

National boundary
Motorway
Major Road

0   100 km

Map © Rough Guides, 1999

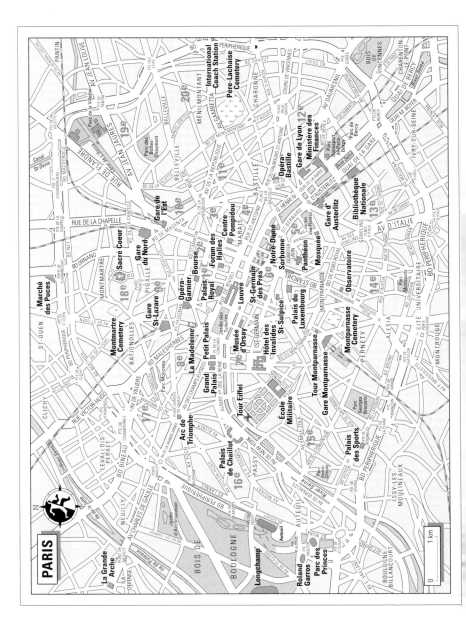

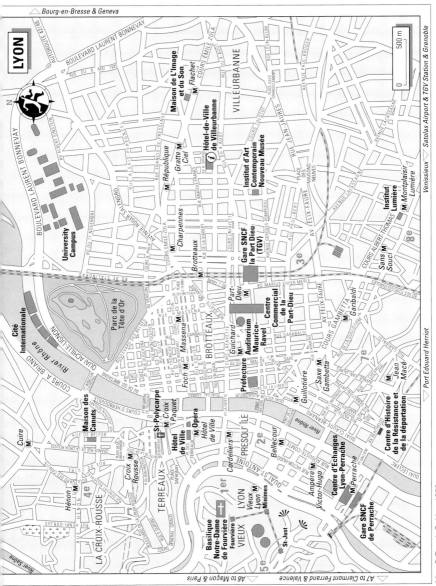

LYON

N

BOULEVARD LAURENT BONNEVAY

RUE DU 8 MAI 1945

AUTOROUTE A42/A6

AV. ALBERT EINSTEIN

BOULEVARD LAURENT BONNEVAY

University Campus

Maison de l'Image et du Son
M Flachet
COURS ÉMILE ZOLA

AVENUE ROGER SALENGRO

BD DU 11 NOVEMBRE

VILLEURBANNE

M République

Gratte M Ciel

Hôtel-de-Ville de Villeurbanne
i

COURS EMILE ZOLA

Charpennes M

Cité Internationale

QUAI ACHILLE LIGNON

River Rhône

Parc de la Tête d'Or

Brotteaux M

Institut d'Art Contemporain
Nouveau Musée

RUE JEAN-JAURÈS

Gare SNCF la Part Dieu (TGV)

3e

Institut Lumière
M Montplaisir Lumière
8e

Sans Souci M

COURS A. BRIAND

BROTTEAUX

Massena M

Part-Dieu M

Centre Commercial de la Part-Dieu

Auditorium Maurice Ravel
Guichard

Foch M

Préfecture M

BD DE STALINGRAD

Saxe M Gambetta

AV. FÉLIX-FAURE

Garibaldi

COURS GAMBETTA

7e

Jean Macé M

Guillotière M

Maison des Canuts
Cuire M

Croix Rousse M

Hénon M

4e

LA CROIX-ROUSSE

GRANDE RUE DE LA CROIX ROUSSE

St-Polycarpe
M Croix Paquet

M Opéra

Hôtel de Ville M

Hôtel de Ville

TERREAUX

Cordeliers M

PRESQU'ÎLE

River Rhône

QUAI ST-ANTOINE

Bellecour M

2e

Ampère M Victor-Hugo

Centre d'Échanges Lyon-Perrache
M Perrache

Gare SNCF de Perrache

Centre d'Histoire et de la Résistance et de la déportation

Basilique Notre-Dame de Fourvière
Fourvière

VIEUX LYON
Vieux M Lyon
Minimes

1er

5e

St-Just

QUAI LECLERC

River Saône

0   500 m

Map © Rough Guides, 1999

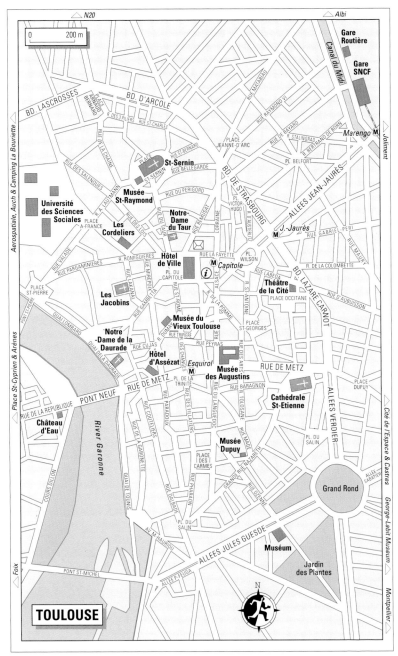

TOULOUSE

Map © Rough Guides, 1999

an elected 65-member council, bringing together parliamentary deputies, regional and general councillors and representatives of mayors.

There are 96 departments within the 22 regions, each governed by a directly elected General Council. In March 1982 state-appointed Regional Prefects were abolished and their executive powers transferred from the state to the presidents of the regional councils. Legislation of 1993 provides for the election every 3 years of half the members of the councils. Elections for 2,009 seats in the General Councils were held in 2 rounds on 20 and 27 March 1994. The electorate was 18,563,056; turn-out was 60·39% at the first round and 58·78% at the second. The PS gained 532 seats, the UDF 446, the RPR 382, various right-wing groups 309, various left-wing groups 171, the Communist Party 145, Greens 7, the National Front 3, others 12.

Elections for the country's 22 regional councils were held on 15 March 1998 and over the next couple of weeks. The vote for the main parties in government (Socialists, Communists and Greens) was 38% and for the moderate right-wing parties (RPR and UDF) 36%. The National Front won 15%. In order to deprive the Left of an overall victory, the Right forged local alliances with the National Front in 5 regions, so as to keep control.

The unit of local government is the *commune*, the size and population of which vary considerably. There were, in 1995, in the 96 metropolitan departments, 36,763 communes (30,919 with fewer than 1,500 inhabitants). The local affairs of the commune are under a Municipal Council, composed of between 9 and 36 members elected by universal suffrage for 6 years. At the last municipal elections in 1995, there were 512,850 municipal councillors. Each municipal council elects a mayor who is both the representative of the commune and agent of the central government. Communes are associated in the *Assemblée des Districts et des Communautés de France*, and also co-operate in inter-commune public enterprise projects, of which there were some 1,200 in 1995.

In Paris the local council *(Conseil de Paris)* is composed of 109 members elected from the 20 *arrondissements*. It combines the functions of departmental General and Municipal Council.

In 1995 the *Pasqua* Law on Guidance for Territorial Management created a new territorial entity, the *pays*. These do not replace administrative divisions, but group regions, departments or communes according to historical, geographical or employment area criteria, with a view to their economic development. Some 200 *pays* had been formed by 1996.

Local revenue is raised from residence, business and property taxes, and amounted to 262,700m. francs in 1995 (250,000m. in 1994).

DEFENCE

Budget

Defence expenditure (in FF):

1995 expenditure	238,432m. (US$47,782m.)
1996 expenditure	237,375m. (US$48,444m.)
1997 expenditure	242,485m. (US$45,752m.)
1998 budget	238,200m. (US $39,700m.)
1999 budget	243,500m. (US $43,482m.)

The budget is frequently quoted without including pensions, i.e. 189,959m. FF for 1999. The above figures include Service pensions. The budget is expected to remain constant until 2002 with procurement accounting for about 86,000m. FF (the 1999 allocation) annually.

Strength of Armed Forces

The active strength of the Armed Forces is:

Nuclear Forces	8,700	
Army	203,200	
Navy	63,300	(includes Naval Air and Marines)
Air Force	78,100	
Total	*353,300*	

The Armed Forces are being reorganized, reducing the active strength to 257,000. Re-organization is due to be complete by 2002. The total strength of the Reserves is about 292,500 (Army, 195,500; Navy, 27,000; Air Force, 70,000). It is intended to establish an all-volunteer Reserve of 100,000, half of which will serve with the Gendarmerie. While on duty, Reservists will enjoy the same status and pay as Regulars.

Paramilitary Forces

The strength of the Gendarmerie is:

Territorial	60,000	
Mobile	17,000	
Schools	5,500	
Republican Guard	4,600	(includes Air Transport and Arsenals)
Overseas	3,100	
Administration	3,000	
Total	**93,400**	

Gendarmerie Reserves number about 139,000.

Conscription

Conscription is for 10 months, with the conversion to fully professional Armed Forces due to be complete by 2002. Of the Armed Forces' strength of 353,300, about 129,250 (37%) are conscripts. Within the

Services approximately 27% of the Central Staff, 44% of the Army, 27% of the Navy and 26% of the Air Force are conscripts. The Gendarmerie of 93,400 includes 13,000 (14%) conscripts.

With the ending of conscription, 18 year-olds are being required to report to one of 220 barracks for a single day of themed defence-related presentations and literacy tests. The 'Call-up for Defence Preparation' will eventually be attended by some 800,000 young men and women each year.

Nuclear Capability

The first of the new nuclear-powered, ballistic-missile submarines (SSBN), *Le Triomphant*, entered service in Sept. 1996 with sister boats due to follow in 1999, 2001 and 2005. *Le Triomphant* is armed with the M45 submarine-launched ballistic missile (SLBM) and new TN75 warheads. A new SLBM, the M51, is due to replace the M45 from about 2010. It is anticipated that there will eventually be 288 100-kiloton warheads for the new boats, replacing a similar number in current service. The 18 silo-based S3D intermediate-range ballistic missiles (IRBM) were deactivated between 1996 and 1998 and are not being replaced. Aircraft are armed with the 300 kiloton Air-Sol Moyenne Portée (ASMP) with a 300 km range. Plans have been announced for an ASMP Plus with a 500 km range. Three squadrons of Mirage 2000N have assumed a 'strategic' role in addition to their 'pre-strategic' one. The aircraft carrier *Charles de Gaulle* has a single squadron of Super Etendard, assumed to have about 10 ASMP, until the Rafale M enters service in 2002. It is estimated that the total ASMP stockpile is 65.

Policy

France remains outside NATO's military structure, having been withdrawn by President de Gaulle in 1966. In 1995 moves by President Chirac to reintegrate France into the military structure ended with

misunderstanding and disagreement with the United States, particularly over the vexed question of the nationality of NATO's Southern
Commander. *De facto* France is integrated into the Alliance, as
witnessed by the French contribution to the Kosovo Campaign and it
is only a matter of time before the matter is resolved *de jure*.

France perceives a need to restrain United States' unilateralism,
seeing Europe as a multiplier of its national power. Central to French
policy is its relationship with Germany and the fear that France could
end up as a second-tier country in a German-run Europe. France is a
leading proponent of a European defence arm. France's military
weight, including a nuclear capability and coupled with membership
of the UN Security Council, acts as a counter-balance to Germany's
economic and political power.

Following the 1996 decision to end conscription, two further
rounds of Armed Forces' reorganization were announced in 1997 and
1998. The 1997 decision included the disbandment of 39 regiments,
preservation of 13 warships and the closure of some airbases and
hospitals. Most of this action has been completed. The 1998 overhaul
addressed the logistics, training and administration of the Armed
Forces. It is intended that the Armed Forces will be smaller, more
mobile and better trained by 2002.

INTERNATIONAL RELATIONS

France is a member of the UN, the Council of Europe, NATO, WEU,
EU, OSCE, OECD and the Pacific Community, and is a signatory to
the Schengen Accord, which abolishes border controls between
Austria, Belgium, Denmark, Finland, France, Germany, Greece,
Iceland, Italy, Luxembourg, the Netherlands, Norway, Portugal, Spain
and Sweden.

At a referendum in Sept. 1992 to approve the ratification of the Maastricht treaty on European union of 7 Feb. 1992, 12,967,498 votes (50·81%) were cast for and 12,550,651 (49·18%) against.

France is the focus of the *Communauté Francophone* (French-speaking Community) which formally links France with many of its former colonies in Africa. A wide range of agreements, both with members of the Community and with other French-speaking countries, extend to economic and technical matters, and in particular to the disbursement of overseas aid.

ECONOMY

Performance

Real GDP growth was estimated at 2·3% in 1997 (1·5% in 1996); a rate of 2·7% was forecast for 1998. Contributory factors to economic growth in 1997 were a strong export market and weaker franc. Total GDP (1996, in US$1): 1,539,000m. (1997 forecast: 1,358,300m.).

A second phase of privatization (the first being in 1986–87) involving some 20 state enterprises was initiated by legislation of May 1993, by which the state retained the right to acquire a 'golden share' to give itself veto powers in the national interest. In 1997 the sale of state assets included nearly a quarter of France Télécom and a majority stake in the CIC banking network. Other sell-offs in the pipeline (in 1998) included Air France (49%) and a controlling stake in the defence electronics giant Thomson-CSF.

France's GNP per capita in 1996 for purchasing power was $21,510.

Budget

In 1997 public spending was cut by an extra 10,000m. francs when the new government came to power in June. The budget for 1998 envisaged no further cuts in public spending (but an increase in line with inflation forecast at 1·5%); and a reduction in the public deficit from 3·1% of GDP in 1997 (dramatically reduced in June from an estimated 3·5% and rising by the acquisition of 22,000m. francs in emergency corporate taxes) to 3% of GDP, which is the uppermost limit of the Maastricht criteria on budget deficits.

Receipts and expenditure in 1m. francs:

	1993	1994	1995	1996	1997
Revenue	1,142,698	1,154,165	1,291,700	1,264,162	1,194,700
Expenditure	1,410,129	1,436,333	1,595,700	1,551,969	1,480,800

In Nov. 1997 receipts were up by 18,700m. francs on the previous year; expenditure was up by 16,500m. The budget deficit at 30 Nov. 1997 was some 325,300m. francs (4,100m. francs less than at 31 Dec. 1996).

Breakdown of revenue and expenditure (in 1m. francs):

Receipts	1994	1995	1996
Income tax	296,328	303,525	314,100
Corporation tax	127,857	145,748	143,200
Other direct taxes	111,148	116,820	136,474
Stamp duty	77,758	83,400	81,745
Customs duties	155,080	158,801	158,986
VAT	648,393	673,216	761,627
Other indirect taxes	41,040	44,707	46,083
Non-fiscal receipts	161,661	150,365	115,564
Expenditure			
Public debt	199,834	198,983	226,369
Administration	506,410	524,275	. . .
Subsidies	406,420	417,531	1,073,496[1]
Civil investments	89,111	86,172	. . .
Defence	242,558	243,456	241,449

[1] Civil expenditure total.

The standard rate of VAT is 20·6% (reduced rate, 5·5%).

Ministère de l'Economie, des Finances et du Plan. *Le Budget de l'Etat: de la Préparation à l'Exécution*. Paris, 1995

Currency

On 1 Jan. 1999 the euro (EUR) became the legal currency in France and the *franc* became a subdivision of it; irrevocable conversion rate 6·55957 francs to 1 euro. The euro, which consists of 100 cents, will not be in circulation until 1 Jan. 2002. There will be 7 euro notes in different colours and sizes denominated in 500, 200, 100, 50, 20, 10 and 5 euros, and 8 coins denominated in 2 and 1 euros, then 50, 20, 10, 5, 2 and 1 cents. Even though notes and coins will not be introduced until 1 Jan. 2002 the euro can be used in banking; by means of cheques, travellers' cheques, bank transfers, credit cards and electronic purses. Banking will be possible in both euros and francs until the franc is withdrawn from circulation – which must be by 1 July 2002.

The franc (FRF) is made up of 100 centimes. Notes in circulation at 29 Jan. 1998: 261,338m. francs. In Feb. 1998 foreign exchange reserves were US$28,035m. and gold reserves were 81·89m. troy oz. The annualized rate of inflation in 1997 was 1·2% (2% in 1996), with a projected fall to 0·9% in 1998.

Franc Zone. 13 former French colonies (Benin, Burkina Faso, Cameroon, Central African Republic, Chad, Comoros, the Republic of the Congo, Côte d'Ivoire, Gabon, Mali, Niger, Senegal and Togo), the former Spanish colony of Equatorial Guinea and the former Portuguese colony of Guinea-Bissau are members of a Franc Zone, the CFA (*Communauté Financière Africaine*). Comoros uses the Comorian franc. From 1948 to 1994, 1 French franc equalled 50 francs CFA. The franc CFA was devalued by 50% on 11 Jan. 1994 and the Comorian franc by 25%. The franc CFP *(Comptoirs Français du Pacifique)* is the common currency of the French dependencies of

French Polynesia, New Caledonia and Wallis and Futuna. It has a parity of CFP francs 18·18 to the French franc.

Banking and Finance

The central bank and bank of issue is the *Banque de France* (*Governor*: Jean-Claude Trichet, appointed 1993), founded in 1800, and nationalized on 2 Dec. 1945. In 1993 it received greater autonomy in line with EU conditions. The Governor is appointed for a 6-year term (renewable once) and heads the 9-member Council of Monetary Policy.

The National Credit Council, formed in 1945 to regulate banking activity and consulted in all political decisions on monetary policy, comprises 45 members nominated by the Government; its president is the Minister for the Economy; its Vice-President is the Governor of the Banque de France.

In 1996 there were 1,445 banks and other credit institutions, including 400 shareholder-owned banks and 342 mutual or savings banks. 4 principal deposit banks were nationalized in 1945, the remainder in 1982; the latter were privatized in 1987. The banking and insurance sectors underwent a flurry of mergers, privatizations, foreign investment, corporate restructuring and consolidation in 1997, in both the national and international fields. Further flotations planned included the sale of the state-owned insurance company GAN (1998) and Crédit Lyonnais (by 2000).

The state savings organization *Caisse Nationale d'Epargne* is administered by the post office on a giro system. There are also commercial savings banks (*caisses d'epargne et de prévoyance*). Deposited funds are centralized by a non-banking body, the *Caisse de Dépôts et Consignations*, which finances a large number of local authorities and state-aided housing projects, and carries an important portfolio of transferable securities.

Banque de France

Founded in 1800, acts as banker to the treasury, issues bank notes, controls credit and money supply and administers France's gold and currency assets. In 1993 the National Assembly approved legalization to make the Banque de France an independent central bank, with a General Council to supervize activities and appoint the principal officials, and a 9-member monetary policy committee, independent of government control, to be in charge of monetary policy.

39 rue Croix des Petits Champs, BP 140-01. 75049 Paris.
Tel: (0)1 42-92-42-92. Fax: (0)1 42-96-04-23.

Caisse des Depôts et Consignations

Founded in 1816. The State Savings Bank manages state saving systems and holds widespread investments in industrial companies.

56 rue de Lille, 75356 Paris. Tel: (0)1 40-49-56-78.
Fax: (0)1 40-49-76-87.

Other Banks

American Express Bank (France) SA

11 rue Scribe, 75009 Paris. Tel: (0)1 47-49-56-78.

Banque CEGR France

21 boulevard Malasherbes, BP 496, 75336 Paris.
Tel: (0)1 42-68-62-00. Fax: (0)1 42-66-35-30.

Banque Caisse de Gestion Mobilière

6 rue des Petit Pères, 75002 Paris. Tel: (0)1-40-20-20-00.
Fax: (0)1-42-86-90-05.

Banque de Bretagne

18 quay Duguay Trouin, 35084 Rennes Cédex. Tel: (0)2 99-01-77-77.
Fax: (0)2 99-01-75-00.

Banque Commerciale pour l'Europe du Nord (Eurobank)

79-81 boulevard Haussemann, 75382 Paris. Tel: (0)1-40-06-43-21.

Fax: (0)1-40-06-48-48.

Banque Française du Crédit Cooperatif

33 rue des Trois Fontanot, BP 211, 92002 Nanterre Cédex.

Tel: (0)1 47-24-85-00. Fax: (0)1 47-24-89-25.

Banque Française de l'Orient

33 rue de Monaceau, 75008 Paris. Tel: (0)1-40-74-33-00.

Fax: (0)1-45-63-98-22.

Banque National de Paris, SA

16 boulevard des Italiens, 75009 Paris. Tel: (0)1 40-14-45-46.

Fax: (0)1 40-14-69-55.

Banque Paribas

3 rue d'Antin, 75002 Paris. Tel: (0)1-42-98-12-34.

Fax: (0)1-42-98-11-42.

Barclays Bank PLC

21 rue Lafitte, 75002 Paris. Tel: (0)1 44-79-79-79.

Fax: (0)1 44-79-75-52.

Caisse Centrale des Banques Populaires

10–12 avenue Winston Churchill, 94677 Charenton Le Pont Cédex. Tel:

(0)1 40-39-30-00. Fax: (0)1 40-39-39-49.

Caisse Nationale de Crédit Agricole

91–93 boulevard Pasteur, 75015 Paris. Tel: (0)1 43-23-52-02.

Fax: (0)1 43-23-20-28.

Centrale de Banque, SA

5 boulevard de la Madeleine, 75001 Paris. Tel: (0)1-44-77-40-00.

Fax: (0)1-42-61-37-40.

Supervisory body
Association Française des Etablissements de Crédit (AFEC)
36 rue Taitbout, 75009 Paris. Tel: (0)1-48-24-34-34.
Fax: (0)1 48-24-13-31.

Banking Association
Association Française des Banques
18 rue La Fayette, 75440 Paris Cédéx 09. Tel: (0)1 48-00-52-52.
Fax: (0)1 42-46-76-40.

Stock Exchange
The Paris 'Bourse' was established in 1725. During the 1980s the Bourse underwent a programme of change and deregulation. Floor-based transactions gave way to a nationwide electronic market with a computerized clearing and settlement system (Relit). The reforms allowed member firms to open their capital to banks, insurance companies and other financial institutions. There are provincial exchanges in Bordeaux, Lille, Lyon, Marseilles, Nancy and Nantes. In 1986 MATIF (the Marché à Terme International de France) opened and is the financial and commodities futures operating independently of the Paris Bourse. In 1987 MONEP (the Marché des Options Negociables de Paris) opened, offering stock and index options operating as part of the Paris Bourse.

Société des Bourses Françaises (SBF) – Bourse de Paris
39 rue Cambon, 75001 Paris. Tel: (0)1 49-27-10-00.
Fax: (0)1 49-27-14-33.

Weights and Measures
The metric system is in general use.

ENERGY AND NATURAL RESOURCES

Environmental Policy

France has a civil nuclear programme which provides 80% of total domestic electricity production. The last tests on nuclear weapons were conducted just before President Jacques Chirac signed the worldwide test ban treaty for France in 1998 (together with the UK).

The most important issues facing France at the moment are forest damage by acid rain, air pollution from industrial and vehicle emissions, water pollution from urban wastes and agricultural run-off.

France has two major tools in the conservation and management of natural areas in France: National Nature Parks and Regional Nature Parks. In 30 years, 30 such parks have been set up. They are funded by contributions from central government. Management and conservation of forests have included working with Finland to instigate ministerial conferences on the protection of European forests.

Three conventions have been signed by France since the Rio summit and Agenda 21 has been adopted. This covers all areas to which thought must be devoted in order to ensure that the patterns of consumption are sustainable and that economic development is reconciled with social and environmental well-being.

Electricity

The state-owned monopoly Electricité de France is responsible for power generation and supply under the Ministry of Industry. Installed capacity was 102·94m. kW in 1994. Electricity production (1995, in 1m. kWh): 470,974, of which 358,600 (76·14%) was nuclear. Hydro-electric power contributes about 20% of total electricity output (80,606m. kWh in 1994). Consumption per capita in 1995 was estimated to be 6,278 kWh. In 1997 it was the European Union's biggest exporter of electricity with 71·4bn. kWh.

France, not rich in natural energy resources, is at the centre of Europe's nuclear energy industry. In 1997 there were 56 nuclear reactors in operation, with a capacity of 58·4m. kW, providing some 72·9% of the electricity output. Nuclear reactors accounted for 38% of total energy consumption in 1994. There were 4 new nuclear plants under construction in 1997, one of which (in western France) was cancelled mid-way through the year and Electricité de France announced that it will not be considering any new plants before 2000. Also in 1997, following concern over its safety, it was decided that the 12-year-old Superphénix plant east of Lyons would be shut down.

Oil and Gas

In 1994, 2·8m. tonnes of crude oil were produced. The greater part came from the Parentis oilfield in the Landes. The importation and distribution of natural gas is the responsibility of the government monopoly Gaz de France. Production of natural gas (1994) was 94·4 petajoules. In 1994, 41·2% of total energy consumption came from oil; 13% from gas.

Minerals

France is a significant producer of nickel, uranium, iron ore, bauxite, potash, crude steel, pig iron, aluminium and coal. Société Le Nickel extracts in New Caledonia and is the world's third largest nickel producer; France is the world's seventh largest uranium producer. The mining sector contributed 1% of GDP in 1994, and employed 0·8% of the workforce.

Coal production (1995): 5·1m. tonnes. Coal power generators contributed 6·2% of total energy consumption in 1994. Coal reserves in Jan. 1996: 139m. tonnes. Production of other principal minerals and metals (1994, in 1,000 tonnes): crude steel, 18,242; iron ore (metal content), 708; pig iron, 12,444; aluminium (unwrought, primary), 481·50; potash salts, 936.

Agriculture

The agricultural sector contributes about 4·6% of GDP, and employs about 4·5% of the workforce, down from 8·5% in 1980. Agriculture accounts for 14·5% of exports and 11·4% of imports.

In 1998 there were 680,000 holdings, compared to over 1m. in 1988. Co-operatives account for between 30-50% of output. In 1990 crop production accounted for 54·4% of total agricultural output; animal production for 45·6%.

Of the total area of France (54·9m. ha), the utilized agricultural area comprised 29·99m. ha in 1996. 18·29m. ha were arable, 10·53m. ha were under pasture, and 1·16m. ha were under permanent crops including vines (0·91m. ha).

Area under cultivation and yield for principal crops:

	Area (1,000 ha)			Produce (1,000 tonnes)		
	1994	*1995*	*1996*	*1994*	*1995*	*1996*
Wheat	4,580	4,744	5,040	30,549	30,879	35,948
Rye	45	46·3	48·6	176	190·7	220·8
Barley	1,405	1,339	1,485	7,646	7,492	9,276
Oats	166	148·8	139·5	685	601·2	621·9
Sugar-beet	437	458·2	456·7	29,037	30,571	30,943
Maize	1,660	1,650	1,733	12,943	12,739	14,529
Sorghum	. . .	45·6	54·7	. . .	256·4	343·1

Production of principal fruit crops (in 1,000 tonnes) as follows:

	1994	*1995*	*1996*		*1994*	*1995*	*1996*
Apples[1]	2,166	2,078	2,019	Melons	330	329	314
Pears	343	320	353	Nuts	27	38	39
Plums	221	299	364	Table grapes	69	107	95
Peaches	528	526	467	Strawberries	83	81	81·2
Apricots	155	100	174	Clementines	22	27	21

[1] Does not include apples for cider-making.

Total area under cultivation and yield of grapes from the vine (1996): 871,038 ha; 7·57m. tonnes. Estimated wine production (1997–98): 56m. hectolitres.

The area under cultivation (and yield) for vegetables in 1996 was as follows: Leaf and stem, 130,544 ha (2·4m. tonnes); fruit vegetables, 39,882 ha (1·5m. tonnes); roots and bulbs, 44,782 ha (1·33m. tonnes); pods, 86,339 ha (657,461 tonnes); beans, lentils and other dry, 10,213 ha (20,449 tonnes).

Livestock (1996, in 1,000): Horses, 337; asses and mules, 13·7; cattle, 20,655; sheep, 10,457; goats, 1,202; pigs, 14,283; poultry, 231,003 (laying hens, 49,324); rabbits, 14,439. Livestock products (1996, in 1,000 tonnes): beef and veal, 1,470; pork, 2,038; lamb and mutton, 152; poultry, 2,103; rabbit, 90; horse, 14; eggs, 1,026 (1995). Milk production: cows', 243,538,646 hectolitres; sheep's, 2,339,865 hectolitres; goats', 4,574,176 hectolitres.

Forestry

Forestry is France's richest natural resource, with a revenue of about 8,000m. francs a year, and accounts for 0·55m. of the workforce. In 1995 forest covered 15·03m. ha (27·3% of the land area). In 1990 the area under forests had been 14·23m. ha, or 25·9% of the land area. 73·7% of forest is private; 26% state-owned. Timber production in 1995 was 46·34m. cu. metres.

Fisheries

In 1996 there were 6,509 fishing vessels totalling 176,356 GRT, and 17,101 fishermen. Catch (1996, in tonnes): 868,572 (fish, 634,894; shellfish and molluscs, 233,678). Sea fishing accounts for approximately 92% of the total catch.

INDUSTRY

The industrial sector contributes around 28% of GDP and employs about 27% of the workforce. In Nov. 1997 capacity utilization in industry was approaching 85%. Chief industries: steel, chemicals, textiles, aircraft, machinery, electronic equipment, tourism, wine and perfume.

Industrial production (1994, in 1,000 tonnes): sulphuric acid, 2,227; caustic soda, 1,561; cement, 20,184. In 1993 (in 1,000 tonnes): sulphur, 1,106; polystyrene, 481; polyvinyl, 1,176; polyethylene, 1,308; wool, 56; cotton, 152; linen, 6; silk, 71.

Food products (1993, in 1,000 tonnes): chocolate, 547; biscuits, 475; sugar, 4,599; fish preparations, 109; jams and jellies, 161; cheese (1994), 1,562.

Engineering production (1994, in 1,000 units): car tyres, 66,744; motor vehicles, 3,176; television sets, 2,796.

Top Ten Companies

Company name	Industry	Revenue ($m.)	World Ranking
AXA-UAP	Insurance	76,869	10
Elf Aquitaine Group	Energy Sources	43,570	28
Renault Group	Automobiles	35,621	39
Total Group	Energy Sources	32,738	44
Suez Lyonnaise Group	Business & Public Services	32,625	45
Peugeot Groupe	Automobiles	32,002	47
Alcatel Alsthom	Electrical & Electronics	31,845	48
Carrefour Group	Merchandising	29,001	56
GAN – Assurances Nationales	Insurance	28,935	58

Labour

According to the Employment Survey of March 1994, there was a working population of 25,136,598 (13,898,272 men and 11,238,326 women); out of an economically active population of 22,074,700, 1,127,300 were engaged in agriculture, forestry and fishing, 1,525,600 in building, 1,422,500 in transport and telecommunications, 1,481,100 in manufacturing industries, 608,300 in banking and insurance, 4,278,700 in services, 2,614,100 in commerce. Some 5m. people work in the public sector at national and local level. It was estimated in 1997 that 51% of households have no-one working in the private sector.

A new definition of 'unemployed' was adopted in Aug. 1995, omitting persons who had worked at least 78 hours in the previous month. Unemployment in 1998 was close to 3m. or 11·5% (1997, 12·5%) of the active population. The long-term jobless accounted for almost 40% of those seeking work. Under an 80% state-funded job creation programme announced in 1997, an extra 350,000 public-sector jobs will be created for the young by 2000.

Conciliation boards (*Conseils de Prud'hommes*) mediate in labour disputes. They are elected for 5-year terms by 2 colleges of employers and employees. In Jan. 1998 the minimum wage (SMIC) was 39·29 francs an hour (6,664 francs a month). SMIC affects about 1·5m. wage-earners. The average annual wage was 114,314 francs in 1994. Retirement age is 60. A 5-week annual holiday is statutory.

In May 1998 the national assembly approved a reduction in the working week from 39 to 35 hours. The main provisions obliged all companies employing more than 20 people to introduce the shorter working week from Jan. 2000 and all the rest from 2002. The law offers a sliding scale of incentives to employers provided that they cut working hours and create extra jobs. A second piece of legislation was planned for 1999 to determine how overtime would be paid, the working hours of salaried staff and the number of hours to be worked during the year. The introduction of a 35-hour working week in 1998 is unlikely to create many jobs but may slow wage claims and increase productivity.

Trade Unions

The main trade union confederations in 1997 were as follows: the Communist-led CGT (Confédération Générale du Travail), founded 1895; the CGT-FO (Confédération Générale du Travail–Force Ouvrière) which broke away from the CGT in 1948; the CFTC (Confédération Française des Travailleurs Chrétiens), founded in 1919 and divided in 1964, with a breakaway group retaining the old name and the main body continuing under the new name of CFDT (Confédération Française Démocratique du Travail); and the CGC (Confédération Générale des Cadres) formed in 1944, which represents managerial and supervisory staff. The main haulage confederation is the FNTR; the leading employers' association is the CNPF, often referred to as the *Patronat*. Unions are not required to publish membership figures, but in 1993 the 2 largest federations, the CGT and CFDT, had an estimated 0·63m. and 0·65m. members respectively.

Although France has the lowest rate of trade union membership in Europe, 9% in 1997 (compared to 29% in Germany, 33% in Britain and over 90% in Sweden), its trade unionists have considerable clout: they run France's welfare system; staff the country's dispute-settling industrial tribunals (*conseils de prud'hommes*); and fix national agreements on wages and working conditions. A union call to strike is invariably answered by more than a union's membership. Nearly 6m. working days were lost in French strikes in 1995 compared to 415,000 in Britain and 247,000 in Germany.

Union Organizations
Confédération Générale du Travail (CGT)
Complexe Immobilier Intersyndical CGT, 263 rue de Paris, 93516
Montreuil.

Tel: (0)1 48-18-80-00. Fax: (0)1 49-88-18-57.

Force Ouvrière
Founded in 1947 as a more moderate alternative to the more left-wing
CGT. Force Ouvrière is a member of the International Confederation
of Free Trade Unions and of the European Trade Union Conference.

141 avenue du Maine, 75680 Paris. Tel: (0)1 40-52-82-00.
Fax: (0)1 40-52-82-82.

Confédération Française Démocratique du Travail (CFDT)
Founded in 1919 – present title and constitution adopted in 1964.
A moderate organization co-ordinating 2,200 trade unions, 102
departmental and overseas unions and 19 affiliated professional
federations.

4 Blvd. de la Villette, 75955 Paris. Tel: (0)1 42-03-80-00.
Fax: (0)1 42-03-81-44.

Employers Organizations
Conseil National du Patronat Français
An employers' organization grouping 1·5m. companies from all
sectors.

31 avenue Pierre 1er de Serbie, 75784 Paris. Tel: (0)1 40-49-44-44.
Fax: (0)1 47-23-47-32.

CHAMBERS OF COMMERCE

There are chambers of commerce in all the larger towns.

Assemblée des Chambres Françaises de Commerce et d'Industrie
45 avenue d'Iéna, 75116 Paris. Tel: (0)1 40-69-37-00.

INTERNATIONAL TRADE

The trade balance showed a surplus of nearly 200,000m. francs in 1997 due to a strong export market, and a drop in imports owing to sluggish domestic demand. Trade balance (1997 estimate, in US$): 19,900m. (1998 forecast, 24,800m.). Main trading partners: Argentina, USA, Austria, Brazil, Canada, Egypt, Finland, Ghana, Japan, Uruguay, Philippines, Poland, Korea (Rep.) and Singapore.

Privatization legislation of May 1993 gave foreign nationals the right to acquire more than 20% of a firm's capital (the previous limit). In 1997, following intense activity on the equity market, approximately one-third of French equity was owned by foreign investors.

Imports and Exports

Total imports (1997, in US$1): 263,919m.; total exports, 285,084m. Principal imports include: oil, machinery and equipment, chemicals, iron and steel, and foodstuffs. Major exports: metals, chemicals, industrial equipment, consumer goods and agricultural products.

Foreign trade by sector (1992, as % of total trade):

	% Imports	% Exports
Agriculture and agri-food	11·6	16·4
Energy	8·6	2·3
Raw materials and semi-products	24·9	23·7
Capital goods	24·2	27·6
Surface transport equipment	11·1	13·9
Consumer goods	16·9	15·3

In 1997 the chief import sources (as % of total imports) were as follows: Germany, 16·6%; Italy, 9·8%; UK, 8·3%; Belgium-Luxembourg, 8%. The chief export markets (as % of total) were: Germany, 15·9%; UK, 10·1%; Italy, 9·3%; Belgium-Luxembourg,

8·1%. Exports to other European Union members constituted 62·9% of the total, and imports from fellow European Union members accounted for 61·0% of all imports.

A Selection of Trade Shows in France

Trade Show	Month	Frequency	Location
Automobile de Lyon Lyon Motor Show Tel: (0)4 72-22-33-44 Tel: (0)4 72-22-32-70 E-mail: foire@sepelcom.com	Oct.	Bi-annual	Lyon Eurexpo
Aéronautique et Espace Paris Air Show Tel: (0)1 53-23-33-33 Fax: (0)1 47-20-00-86 E-mail: siae@salon-du-bourget.fr	June	Bi-annual	Paris Le Bourget
Agriculture International Tel: (0)1 49-09-60-00 Fax: (0)1 49-09-51-58	Feb.	Annual	Paris expo Porte de Versailles
Amélioration Habitat Foire de Paris Tel: (0)1 49-09-60-00 Fax: (0)1 49-09-51-58	April/May	Annual	Paris expo Porte de Versailles
Artisans et Créations Foire de Paris Tel: (0)1 49-09-60-00 Fax: (0)1 49-09-51-58	April/May	Annual	Paris expo Porte de Versailles

Conforexpo Autumn Consumer Exhibition Tel: (0)5 56-11-99-00 Fax: (0)5 56-11-99-99	Nov.	Annual	Bordeaux Lac
Equita'Lyon Horse World Show Tel: (0)4 78-39-18-81 Fax: (0)4 78-29-06-58	Nov.	Annual	Lyon Eurexpo
Cannes International Boat Show Tel: (0)1 42-89-41-04 Fax: (0)1 45-61-12-00	Sept.	Annual	Cannes Vieux port
Foire de Bordeaux Tel: (0)5 56-11-99-00 Fax: (0)5 56-11-99-99	May	Annual	Bordeaux Lac
Foire de Nice Tel: (0)4 92-00-20-80 Fax: (0)4 93-56-49-77	March	Annual	Nice
Grand Pavois International Water Boat Show Tel: (0)5 46-44-46-39 Fax: (0)5 46-45-32-24 E-mail: pavois@club-internet.fr	Sept.	Annual	La Rochelle
Habitat et Deco de Besançon Ideal Home Exhibition Tel: (0)3 81-41-08-09 Fax: (0)3 81-52-18-36	Oct.	Annual	Besançon

Livre et Multimedia Book and multimedia show Tel: (0)1 41-90-47-47 Fax: (0)1 41-90-47-00	March	Annual	Paris expo Porte de Versailles
Marché International du Film/Mif Tel: (0)1 45-61-66-09 Fax: (0)1 45-61-97-59	May	Annual	Cannes Palais du Festivals
Nautique International Tel: (0)1 41-90-47-47 Fax: (0)1 41-90-47-00	Dec.	Annual	Paris expo Porte de Versailles
Sport Show France Tel: (0)1 41-90-47-47 Fax: (0)1 41-90-47-00	June	Annual	Paris expo Porte de Versailles
Top Res Travel & Tourism Trade Show Tel: (0)1 42-50-21-35 Fax: (0)1 47-56-50-67	Sept.	Annual	Deauville Hippodrome de la Touques
Vinexpo International Wine & Spirits Exhibition Tel: (0)5 56-56-00-22 Fax: (0)5 56-79-35-58	June	Bi-Annual	Bordeaux Lac

COMMUNICATIONS

Roads

In 1997 there were 806,000 km of road, including 7,100 km of motorway. France has the densest road network in the world, and the longest in the EU. Around 90% of all freight is transported by road. In 1996 there were 24·4m. private cars and 4·9m. commercial vehicles (3·62m. trucks, about 42,000 buses and 0·87m. motorcycles and scooters). The average distance travelled by a passenger car in the year 1996 was 14,000 km. In 1996 there were 8,080 road deaths, down from 9,083 in 1992.

Rules of the Road

Driving in France is on the right-hand side of the road.

Unless otherwise indicated, priority is given to cars coming from the right.

Unless otherwise indicated (or in adverse weather conditions), speed limits are:-

Motorways: (Autoroutes) 130 km/h

Dual carriageways and non-toll motorways: 110 km/h

Other non-urban roads: 90 km/h

Built up areas: 50 km/h

The wearing of seatbelts is compulsory and children under 10 years are not allowed to travel in the front seat of the car.

Random breath tests are frequent.

Rail

In 1938 all the independent railway companies were merged with the existing state railway system in a Société Nationale des Chemins de Fer Français (SNCF), which became a public industrial and commercial establishment in 1983. Legislation came into effect in 1997 which vested ownership of the railway infrastructure (track and signalling) in a newly established public corporation, the National Railway Network (RFN). The RFN is funded by payments for usage from the SNCF, government and local subventions and authority capital made available by the state derived from the proceeds of privatization. The SNCF remains responsible for maintenance and management of the rail network. The legislation also envisages the establishment of regional railway services which receive funds previously given to the SNCF as well as a state subvention. These regional bodies negotiate with SNCF for the provision of suitable services for their area. SNCF is the most heavily indebted and subsidized (38,000m. francs a year) company in France.

In 1997 SNCF totalled 33,769 km of track (one third of it electrified); it had an annual capacity of 58bn. passenger-km and 45bn. freight tonne-km. High-speed TGV lines link Paris to the south and west of France, and Paris and Lille to the Channel Tunnel (Eurostar). The high-speed TGV line appeared in 1983; it had 1,860 km of track in 1997, and another 4,400 km planned by 2015. Services from London through the Channel Tunnel began operating in 1994.

The Paris transport network consisted in 1993 of 202 km of metro, 352 km of regional express railways, 9·1 km of light rail and 7 km of passenger stock. There are metros in Lille (29 km), Lyons (20·8 km), Toulouse (10 km) and Marseilles (19·5 km), and tram/light railway networks in Grenoble (14·6 km), Lille (23 km), Marseilles (3 km), Nantes (16·5 km), Rouen (17 km), St Étienne (7 km) and Strasbourg (11·4 km).

Société Nationale des Chemins de Fer Français (SNCF)

86–88 rue St. Lazare, 75436 Paris. Tel: (0)1 53-25-60-00. Fax: (0)1 53-25-61-08.

Regie Autonome des Transports Parisien (RATP)

54 quai de la Rapee, 75599 Paris. Tel: (0)1 44-68-20-20. Fax: (0)1 44-68-31-60.

Civil Aviation

The main international airports are at Paris (Charles de Gaulle), Paris (Orly), Bordeaux (Mérignac), Lyons (Satolas), Marseilles-Provence, Nice-Côte d'Azur, Strasbourg (Entzheim), Toulouse (Blagnac) and Nantes (Atlantique). The following had international flights to only a few destinations in 1998: Brest, Caen, Carcassonne, Clermont-Ferrand, Deauville, Le Havre, Le Touquet, Lille, Pau, Rennes, Rouen and Saint-Étienne. The national airline is Air France. In 1995 it flew 349·9m. km, carrying 49,520,000 passengers (36,840,000 on domestic flights). In 1996 Charles de Gaulle airport handled 31,426,903 passengers (28,665,270 on international flights) and 886,114 tonnes of freight, Orly handled 27,333,472 passengers (16,742,976 on domestic flights) and 246,371 tonnes of freight, and Nice-Côte d'Azur handled 6,543,000 passengers (4,154,000 on domestic flights). Marseilles-Provence was the leading provincial airport in 1996 for freight, with 44,055 tonnes.

Airport Authority

Aéroports de Paris

The body in charge of Paris airports:

291 boulevard de Raspail, 75675 Paris. Tel: (0)1 43-35-70-00.
Fax: (0)1 43-35-72-19.

Airlines

Air France (head office)

45 rue de Paris, 95747 Roissy. Tel: (0)1 41-56-78-00.
Fax: (0)1 41-56-70-20.

Airlines Associations

Chambre Syndicale du Transport Aérien (CTSA)

Founded in 1946 to represent French Airlines at national level.

28 rue de Chateaudun, 75009 Paris. Tel: (0)1 45-26-23-24.

Fédération Nationale de l'Aviation Marchande (FNAM)
28 rue de Chateaudun, 75009 Paris. Tel: (0)1 45-26-23-24.

Shipping

The merchant fleet of ocean-going steam and motor ships totalling 1,000 gross tonnes or more (excluding special ships such as cable, icebreakers, etc.) comprised 65 vessels of 1,564,000 GRT in Jan. 1996. In 1993 from a total of 215 vessels (all sizes; GRT: 3,928,000), 212m. tonnes of cargo were unloaded, including 130m. tonnes of crude and refined petroleum products, 93m. tonnes were loaded; total passenger traffic was 29·2m. Chief ports: Marseilles, Le Havre, Nantes, Bordeaux and Rouen.

Conseil National des Communautés Portuaires

Central independent consultative body for ports and port authorities.

34 rue de la Fédération, 75015 Paris. Tel: (0)1 40-81-71-04.

Inland Waterways

France has extensive inland waterways. Canals are administered by the public authority, France Navigable Waterways (FVN). In 1993 there were 8,500 km of navigable rivers, waterways and canals (of which 1,647 km were accessible to vessels over 3,000 tons), with a total traffic of 59·8m. tonnes.

Voies Navigables de France

Founded in 1991 to manage and develop France's inland waterways.

175 rue Ludovic Boutleux, BP 820, 62408 Béthune. Tel: (0)3 21-63-24-24.

Telecommunications

France Télécom became a limited company on 1 Jan. 1997. In 1997, 33·7m. telephone main lines (575 for every 1,000 inhabitants) and

4·3m. mobile telephones were in use. In 1995 there were 1·7m. fax machines (including 0·4m. in working homes); 7·8m. PCs (equivalent to 134 per 1,000 persons); and 6·5m. Minitel videotext terminals were rented out by France Télécom. There were around 2·5m. Internet users in May 1998 – just over 4% of the population.

France Télécom
6 place d'Alleray, 75505 Paris. Tel: (0)1 44-44-89-34. Fax: (0)1 47-51-32-64.

Postal Services
There were 16,919 post offices in 1994. In 1995 a total of 24,391m. pieces of mail were processed, or 419 items per person. La Poste is a public enterprise under autonomous management responsible for mail delivery and financial services.

SOCIAL INSTITUTIONS

Justice
The system of justice is divided into 2 jurisdictions: the judicial, and the administrative. Within the judicial jurisdiction are common law courts including 473 lower courts (*tribunaux d'instance*, 11 in overseas departments), 186 higher courts (*tribunaux de grande instance*, 5 *tribunaux de première instance* in the overseas territories), and 454 police courts (*tribunaux de police*, 11 in overseas departments).

The *tribunaux d'instance* are presided over by a single judge. The *tribunaux de grande instance* usually have a collegiate composition, but may be presided over by a single judge in some civil cases. The *tribunaux de police*, presided over by a judge on duty in the *tribunal d'instance*, deal with petty offences (*contraventions*); correctional chambers (*chambres correctionelles*, of which there is at least 1 in each *tribunal de grande instance*) deal with graver offences (*délits*), including cases involving imprisonment up to 5 years. Correctional chambers normally consist of 3 judges of a *tribunal de grande instance* (a single judge in some cases). Sometimes in cases of *délit*, and in all cases of more serious *crimes*, a preliminary inquiry is made in secrecy by one of 569 examining magistrates (*juges d'instruction*), who either dismisses the case or sends it for trial before a public prosecutor.

Within the judicial jurisdiction are various specialized courts, including 227 commercial courts (*tribunaux de commerce*), composed of tradesmen and manufacturers elected for 2 years initially, and then for 4 years; 271 conciliation boards (*conseils de prud'hommes*), composed of an equal number of employers and employees elected for 5 years to deal with labour disputes; 437 courts for settling rural landholding disputes (*tribunaux paritaires des baux ruraux*, 11 in overseas departments); and 116 social security courts (*tribunaux des affaires de sécurité sociale*).

When the decisions of any of these courts are susceptible of appeal, the case goes to one of the 35 courts of appeal (*cours d'appel*), composed each of a president and a variable number of members. There are 104 courts of assize (*cours d'assises*), each composed of a president who is a member of the court of appeal, and 2 other magistrates, and assisted by a lay jury of 9 members. These try crimes involving imprisonment of over 5 years. The decisions of the courts of appeal and the courts of assize are final. However, the Court of Cassation (*cour de cassation*) has discretion to verify if the law has been correctly interpreted and if the rules of procedure have been followed exactly. The Court of Cassation may annul any judgment, following which the cases must be retried by a court of appeal or a court of assizes.

The administrative jurisdiction exists to resolve conflicts arising between citizens and central and local government authorities.

It consists of 34 administrative courts (*tribunaux administratifs*, 7 in overseas departments and territories) and 5 administrative courts of appeal (*cours administratives d'appel*). The Council of State is the final court of appeal in administrative cases, though it may also act as a court of first instance.

Cases of doubt as to whether the judicial or administrative jurisdiction is competent in any case are resolved by a *Tribunal de conflits* composed in equal measure of members of the Court of Cassation and the Council of State. In 1997 the new government restricted its ability to intervene in individual cases of justice.

Penal code. A revised penal code came into force on 1 March 1994, replacing the *Code Napoléon* of 1810. Penal institutions consist of: (1) *maisons d'arrêt*, where persons awaiting trial as well as those condemned to short periods of imprisonment are kept; (2) punishment institutions – (a) central prisons (*maisons centrales*) for those sentenced to long imprisonment, (b) detention centres for offenders showing promise of rehabilitation, and (c) penitentiary centres, establishments combining (a) and (b); (3) hospitals for the sick. Special attention is being paid to classified treatment and the rehabilitation and vocational re-education of prisoners including work in open-air and semi-free establishments. Juvenile delinquents go before special judges in 138 (11 in overseas departments and territories) juvenile courts (*tribunaux pour enfants*); they are sent to public or private institutions of supervision and re-education.

The first Ombudsman (*Médiateur*) was appointed for a 6-year period in Jan. 1973. The present incumbent is Jacques Pelletier (app. 1992).

Capital punishment was abolished in Aug. 1981. In metropolitan France the detention rate on 1 Jan. 1997 was 88·3 prisoners per 100,000 population, up from 50 per 100,000 in 1975. The average period of detention in 1997 was 8·1 months. The principal offences committed were: theft, 28%; drug-related offences, 18%; rape and

other sexual assaults, 18%. The population of the 187 penal
establishments (3 for women) in Oct. 1998 was 55,155 men and
2,303 women, giving a total of 57,458.

Weston, M., *English Reader's Guide to the French Legal System*. Oxford, 1991

Religion

A law of 1905 separated church and state. In 1996 there were 95
Roman Catholic dioceses in metropolitan France and 112 bishops. In
1992 there were 43·77m. Roman Catholics (over 75% of the population), 0·8m. Protestants and 1·72m. Moslems.

France is primarily a Roman Catholic country but as with other
developed European countries there has been a steady decline in
the number of people attending church (only approximately 14% of
the population attend mass regularly). The priesthood has also
suffered a decline in the number of vocations (there are only about
100 new recruits to the priesthood annually). After the Vatican
Council radically modernized and changed the structure and liturgy
of the church, a French Abbé, Monsignor Lefebvre, broke away from
the rule of Rome and established his own seminary to ordain priests
and follow the old teachings and rites of the church (mainly the
Tridentine Latin Mass). In France a civil wedding must be held at the
couple's local Mairie in addition to any church service which is
optional and has no legal significance. Of the 950,000 French
Protestants, the Calvinist Reformed Church has the most members
and the only women priests in France are to be found in this church.
Other Protestants include Lutherans, Evangelicals, Adventists,
Pentecostalists, etc. There are approximately 750,000 Jews in
France (Judaism has been represented in France since the first
century AD) although 60,000 French Jews have emigrated to Israel
since the end of World War II. There are 4m. practitioners of Islam on
French soil, many of whom are immigrants who arrived during the
1950s and 1960s.

Religious Organizations

Conseils d'Eglises Chrétiennes en France: 80 rue de l'Abbé-Carton, 75014 Paris. Tel: (0)1 45-42-00-39. Fax: (0)1 45-42-03-07.

Founded in 1987, an ecumenical organization with 21 members representing all Christian Denominations.

Conférence des Evêques de France (Bishops' Conference): 106 rue du Bac, 75341 Paris. Tel: (0)1 45-49-70. Fax: (0)1 45-48-13-39.

Fédération Protestante de France: 47 rue de Clichy, 75311 Paris. Tel: (0)1 44-53-47-00. Fax: (0)1 42-81-40-01.

The federation represents various Protestant Churches in France.

Administration of Russian Orthodox Churches in Europe: 12 rue Daru, 75008 Paris. Tel: (0)1 46-22-38-91.

Represents the 100,000 Russian Orthodox believers in France.

Greek Orthodox Church: Cathedral of St. Stéphane, 7 rue Georges Bizet. 75116 Paris. Tel: (0)1 47-20-82-35. Fax: (0)1 47-20-83-15.

Represents the 50,000 Greek Orthodox believers in France.

Archdeacon of France: 7 rue Auguste Vacquerie. 75116 Paris. Tel: (0)1 47-20-22-51.

Part of the Church of England Diocese of Gibraltar representing the Anglican Communion in France.

Institut Musulman de la Grande Mosquée de Paris: 2 place du Puits de l'Ermite, 75005 Paris. Tel: (0)1 45-35-97-33.

Cultural, diplomatic, social, judicial and religious sections, research and information for Muslims in France.

Consistoire Central – Union des Communautés Juives de France 19 rue Saint Georges, 75009 Paris. Tel: (0)1 49-70-88-00. Fax: (0)1 42-81-03-66.

170 Jewish associations and the headquarters of the Chief Rabbi in France.

Charities

Le Secours Catholique (Caritas France) has 68,000 volunteers.

Les Chiffoniers d'Emmaüs, founded by Abbé Pierre, helps the underprivileged and aims at the eradication of poverty.

Education

The primary, secondary and higher state schools constitute the 'Université de France'. Its Supreme Council of 84 members has deliberative, administrative and judiciary functions, and as a consultative committee advises respecting the working of the school system; the inspectors-general are in direct communication with the Minister. For local education administration France is divided into 25 academic areas, each of which has an Academic Council whose members include a certain number elected by the professors or teachers. The Academic Council deals with all grades of education. Each is under a Rector, and each is provided with academy inspectors, 1 for each department.

Compulsory education is provided for children of 6–16. The educational stages are as follows:

1. Non-compulsory pre-school instruction for children aged 2–5, to be given in infant schools or infant classes attached to primary schools.

2. Compulsory elementary instruction for children aged 6–11, to be given in primary schools and certain classes of the *lycées*. It consists of 3 courses: preparatory (1 year), elementary (2 years), intermediary (2 years). Physically or mentally handicapped children are cared for in special institutions or special classes of primary schools.

3. Lower secondary education (*Enseignement du premier cycle du Second Degré*) for pupils aged 11–15, consists of 4 years of study in the *lycées* (grammar schools), *Collèges d'Enseignement Technique* or *Collèges d'Enseignement Général*.

4. Upper secondary education (*Enseignement du second cycle du Second Degré*) for pupils aged 15–18: (1) *Long, général* or

professionel provided by the *lycées* and leading to the *baccalauréat* or to the *baccalauréat de technicien* after 3 years; and (2) *Court*, professional courses of 3, 2 and 1 year are taught in the *lycées d'enseignement professionel*, or the specialized sections of the *lycées*, CES or CEG.

The following table shows the number of schools in 1994–95 and the numbers of pupils in full-time education:

	State Schools	State Pupils	Private Schools	Private Pupils
Nursery	18,646	5,597,600	343	897,300
Primary	35,618		5,626	
Secondary	7,501	4,327,200	3,711	1,142,000

Higher education is provided by the state free of charge in the universities and in special schools, and by private individuals in the free faculties and schools. Legislation of 1968 redefined the activities and working of universities. Bringing several disciplines together, 780 units for teaching and research (*UER–Unités d'Enseignement et de Recherche*) were formed which decided their own teaching activities, research programmes and procedures for checking the level of knowledge gained. They and the other parts of each university must respect the rules designed to maintain the national standard of qualifications. The UERs form the basic units of the 69 state universities and 3 national polytechnic institutes (with university status), which are grouped into 25 *Académies*. There are also 5 Catholic universities in Paris, Angers, Lille, Lyons and Toulouse; and private universities. There were 1,475,181 students at state universities (1993–94); 21,355 at private universities (1991–92).

Outside the university system, higher education (academic, professional and technical) is provided by over 400 schools and institutes, including the 177 *Grandes Écoles*, which are highly selective public or private institutions offering mainly technological or commercial curricula. These have an annual output of about 17,000 graduates, and in 1994–95 there were also 71,271 students in preparatory classes leading to the *Grandes Écoles;* in 1993–94, 232,844 were registered in the Sections de Techniciens Supérieurs, 71,273 in the Écoles d'Ingénieurs.

Adult literacy rate: 99·0%.

In 1993 total expenditure on education came to 5·8% of GNP and represented 10·4% of total government expenditure.

Health

Ordinances of 1996 created a new regional régime of hospital administration and introduced a system of patients' records to prevent abuses of public health benefits. In 1995 there were 160,235 doctors (equivalent to 1 for every 362 persons), 39,284 dentists, 53,085 pharmacists, 330,943 nurses and 11,957 midwives; and 3,810 hospitals, with a provision of 118 beds per 10,000 population.

Welfare

An order of 4 Oct. 1945 laid down the framework of a comprehensive plan of Social Security and created a single organization which superseded the various laws relating to social insurance, workmen's compensation, health insurance, family allowances, etc. All previous matters relating to Social Security are dealt with in the Social Security Code, 1956; this has been revised several times. The Chamber of Deputies and Senate, meeting as Congress on 19 Feb. 1996, adopted an important revision of the Constitution giving parliament powers to review annually the funding of social security (previously managed by the trade unions and employers' associations), and to fix targets for expenditure in the light of anticipated receipts.

In 1997, 6m. people were dependent on the welfare system, which accounted for more than a quarter of GDP (US$333,000m.). The Social Security budget had a deficit of some 17,000m. francs in 1996, and a cumulative debt (1992–96) of 250,000m. francs. A special levy, the new social debt repayment tax (RDS), at 0·5% on all incomes including pensions and unemployment benefit, has been introduced to clear the cumulative debt. A modest reform of the system was announced in June 1997 which will include a review of all welfare benefits.

Contributions. The general social security contribution (CSG) introduced in 1991 was raised by 4% to 7·5% in 1997 by the Jospin administration in an attempt to dramatically reduce the deficit on social security spending, effectively almost doubling the CSG. All wage-earning workers or those of equivalent status are insured regardless of the amount or the nature of the salary or earnings. The funds for the general scheme are raised mainly from professional contributions, these being fixed within the limits of a ceiling and calcu-lated as a percentage of the salaries. The calculation of contributions payable for family allowances, old age and industrial injuries relates only to this amount; on the other hand, the amount payable for sickness, maternity expenses, disability and death is calculated partly within the limit of the 'ceiling' and partly on the whole salary. These contributions are the responsibility of both employer and employee, except in the case of family allowances or industrial injuries, where they are the sole responsibility of the employer.

Self-employed Workers. From 17 Jan. 1948 allowances and old-age pensions were paid to self-employed workers by independent insurance funds set up within their own profession, trade or business. Schemes of compulsory insurance for sickness were instituted in 1961 for farmers, and in 1966, with modifications in 1970, for other non-wage-earning workers.

Social Insurance. The orders laid down in Aug. 1967 ensure that the whole population can benefit from the Social Security Scheme; at pre-sent all elderly persons who have been engaged in the professions, as well as the surviving spouse, are entitled to claim an old-age benefit.

Sickness Insurance refunds the costs of treatment required by the insured and the needs of dependants.

Maternity Insurance covers the costs of medical treatment relating to the pregnancy, confinement and lying-in period; the beneficiaries being the insured person or the spouse.

Insurance for Invalids is divided into 3 categories: (1) those who are capable of working; (2) those who cannot work; (3) those who, in addition, are in need of the help of another person. According to the category, the pension rate varies from 30 to 50% of the average salary for the last 10 years, with additional allowance for home help for the third category.

Old-Age Pensions for workers were introduced in 1910 and are now fixed by the Social Security Code of 28 Jan. 1972. Since 1983 people who have paid insurance for at least 37½ years (150 quarters) receive at 60 a pension equal to 60% of basic salary. People who have paid insurance for less than 37½ years but no less than 15 years can expect a pension equal to as many 1/150ths of the full pension as their quarterly payments justify. In the event of death of the insured person, the husband or wife of the deceased person receives half the pension received by the latter. Compulsory supplementary schemes ensure benefits equal to 70% of previous earnings.

Family Allowances. A controversial programme of means-testing for Family Allowance was introduced in 1997 by the new administration. The Family Allowance benefit system comprises: (a) Family allowances proper, equivalent to 25·5% of the basic monthly salary for 2 dependent children, 46% for the third child, 41% for the fourth child, and 39% for the fifth and each subsequent child; a supplement equivalent to 9% of the basic monthly salary for the second and each subsequent dependent child more than 10 years old, and 16% for each dependent child over 15 years. (b) Family supplement for persons with at least 3 children or one child aged less than 3 years. (c) Ante-natal grants. (d) Maternity grant is equal to 260% of basic salary.

Increase for multiple births or adoptions, 198%; increase for birth or adoption of third or subsequent child, 457%. (e) Allowance for specialized education of handicapped children. (f) Allowance for orphans. (g) Single parent allowance. (h) Allowance for opening of school term. (i) Allowance for accommodation, under certain circumstances. (j) Minimum family income for those with at least 3 children. Allowances (b), (g), (h) and (j) only apply to those whose annual income falls below a specified level.

Workmen's Compensation. The law passed by the National Assembly on 30 Oct. 1946 forms part of the Social Security Code and is administered by the Social Security Organization. Employers are invited to take preventive measures. The application of these measures is supervised by consulting engineers (assessors) of the local funds dealing with sickness insurance, who may compel employers who do not respect these measures to make additional contributions; they may, in like manner, grant rebates to employers who have in operation suitable preventive measures. The injured person receives free treatment, the insurance fund reimburses the practitioners, hospitals and suppliers chosen freely by the injured. In cases of temporary disablement, the daily payments are equal to half the total daily wage received by the injured. In case of permanent disablement, the injured person receives a pension, the amount of which varies according to the degree of disablement and the salary received during the past 12 months.

Unemployment Benefits vary according to circumstances (full or partial unemployment) which are means-tested.

Ambler, J. S. (ed.) *The French Welfare State: Surviving Social and Ideological Change.* New York Univ. Press, 1992

CULTURE

Avignon is one of 9 European Cities of Culture in the year 2000, along with Bergen (Norway), Bologna (Italy), Brussels (Belgium), Helsinki (Finland), Kraków (Poland), Prague (Czech Republic), Reykjavík (Iceland) and Santiago de Compostela (Spain). The title attracts large European Union grants.

Broadcasting

The broadcasting authority (an independent regulatory commission) is the *Conseil Supérieur de l'Audiovisuel (CSA)*. Public radio is provided by Radio France which broadcasts nationwide on *France Info, France Inter, France Musique, France Culture, Radio Bleue* and *Le Mouv'* and, locally, via 39 radio stations. In Oct. 1998, there were 3,229 private local radio stations. An external service, *Radio-France Internationale*, was founded in 1931 (as 'Poste Coloniale'), and broadcasts in 20 languages.

Two of the state-owned TV channels are partly financed by advertising – *FR2* and *FR3* – and there are 4 private terrestrial channels. Colour is by SECAM. TV broadcasts must contain at least 60% EU-generated programmes and 50% of these must be French.

There were about 58m. radio receivers in use in 1997; and 34·25m. TV sets (1995).

State Controlled Television

There are 3 state controlled national TV channels. Until the mid-1990s, French state controlled television was protected from competition by legislation but under pressure from the private sector and cable companies, the 2 public channels were re-named and France Television was created to manage them. The third channel, La Cinquième, started up in 1994, mainly as an education service.

France Télévision

Founded in 1992. The supervisory body for the 3 state-controlled national television channels.

7 esplanade Henri de France, 75907 Paris Cedex 15.

Tel: (0)1 56-22-60-00. Web: www.francetv.fr

Société Nationale de Télévision – France 2 (F2)

Founded 1975 as Antenne 2 (A2). Broadcasts general programmes.

7 esplanade Henri de France, 75907 Paris Cedex 15.

Tel: (0)1 56-22-60-00 Web: www.france2.fr

Société Nationale de Programmes – France 3 (F3)

Founded 1975 as France Regions 3 (FR3), broadcasting general and regional programmes (from 13 regional stations).

7 esplanade Henri de France, 75907 Paris Cedex 15.

Tel: (0)1 56-22-60-00. Web: www.france3.fr

La Cinquième

Founded 1994, broadcasting mostly educational programmes.

10–14 rue Horace Vernet, 92136 Issy-les-Moulineaux.

Tel: (0)1 41-46-55-55. Web: www.lacinquieme.fr

Private Television

There are 4 main terrestrial private television channels broadcasting nationwide. TF1, a former state channel privatized in 1987; M6, established in 1987; Arte, a joint Franco–German cultural channel; and Canal-Plus, a subscription channel.

TF1 (Télévision Française 1)

Founded 1975 – general programming.

1 quai du Pont du Jour, 92656 Boulogne. Tel: (0)2 41-41-12-34.

Web: www.tf1.fr

M6 (Métropole Télévision)

Founded 1986, specializing in drama, music and magazines.

89 avenue Charles de Gaulle, 92575 Neuilly-sur-Seine.

Tel: (0)1 41-92-66-66. Web: www.m6.fr

Arte

Founded 1990 and owned 50/50 by Arte–Deutschland and La Septe Arte, broadcasting arts and educational programmes nationwide.

2a rue de la Fonderie, 67080 Strasbourg. Tel: (0)3 88-14-22-22. Web: www.arte.fr

Canal Plus

Founded 1984, broadcasting coded programmes financed by audience subscription specializing in drama, cinema and sport.

85–89 quai André Citroën, 75711 Paris Cedex 15.

Tel: (0)1 44-25-10-00 Web: www.cplus.fr

Satellite and Cable Television

Satellite

France has been broadcasting via satellite since 1984 with a combined service relaying programmes from Belgian and Swiss as well as French satellites. More satellites have been added including TDF1 and TDF2 broadcasting for Arte, Canal Plus and Radio France. Télécom A and Télécom B transmit for the principal TV stations and from 1995, Astra, Eutelsat and Télécom satellites have been broadcasting to the majority of households able to receive television. Digital Television arrived in 1996 and 3 new satellites, Canal Satellite, Télévision par Satellite and AB Sat, were launched.

Cable

In addition to specialized French national channels, foreign channels are also transmitted to approximately 1·5m. French households via cable.

CINEMA

There were 4,365 screens in 1995; attendances totalled 130·1m. (126m. in 1994); 115 full-length films were made in 1994. Around 360 new screens were to be opened between 1998 and 2000.

PRESS

There were about 80 daily papers (10 nationals, 70 provincials) in 1997. Top dailies: *L'Équipe*; *Le Monde*; *Le Parisien-Aujourd'hui*; *Le Figaro-L'Aurore*; *Libération*; *France-Soir*; *Ouest France*; *Le Progrès*; *Centre France*; *Sud Ouest*; *Voix du Nord*. The *Journal de Dimanche* is the only national Sunday paper. In 1995, total daily press circulation was 13·6m. copies, up from 10·3m. in 1980.

Newspapers

Le Monde

Founded 1944. A liberal, independent daily newspaper with a circulation of 370,000. Monthly supplements: Le Monde Diplomatique, Le Monde de l'Education, Le Monde de Débats, Le Monde de Philatelistes, etc.

21 bis, rue Claude-Bernard, 75242 Paris. Tel: (0)1 42-17-20-00. Fax: (0)1 42-17-21-21. Web site: www.lemonde.fr

L'Equipe

Founded 1946. France's sporting paper, with a circulation of nearly 400,000.

4 rue Bourget-de-l'Isle, 92137 Issy-les-Moulineaux. Tel: (0)1 40-93-20-20. Fax: (0)1 40-93-20-08.

Le Figaro

Founded 1828. A morning paper covering morning news, literary reviews, etc. Magazine on Saturdays plus three weekly supplements.

37 rue du Louvre, 75081 Paris. Tel: (0)1 42-21-62-00.
Fax: (0)1 42-21-64-05. Web site: www.lefigaro.fr

International Herald Tribune

Founded in 1887. US-based English language daily newspaper.
Circulation 194,000.

181 avenue Charles de Gaulle, 92521 Neuilly-sur-Seine.
Tel: (0)1 41-43-93-00. Fax: (0)1 41-43-93-93.
Web site: www.iht.com

France-Dimanche

Founded 1946. Popular Sunday newspaper. Circulation 640,000.

10 rue Thierry le Luron, 92592 Levallois-Perret.
Tel: (0)1 41-34-85-51. Fax: (0)1 41-34-85-81.

Le Journal Officiel de la République Française

Founded 1870. The official journal of the Government. Publishes
laws, decrees, parliamentary proceedings and economic bulletins.

26 rue Desaix, 75727 Paris. Tel: (0)1 40-58-75-00.
Fax: (0)1 45-79-17-84.

L'Humanité

Founded 1904 (by Jean Jaurès). The only paper in France which is
the official organ of a political party (the French Communist Party).
Circulation 118,000.

32 rue Jean Jaurès, 93528 Saint-Denis. Tel: (0)1 49-22-72-72.
Fax: (0)1 49-22-73-00.

Current Affairs Magazines

L'Express

Founded 1953. Weekly current affairs. Circulation 430,000.

61 avenue Hoche, 75411 Paris. Tel: (0)1 40-54-30-00.
Fax: (0)1 42-67-72-93. Web: www.lexpress.fr

Le Nouvel Observateur

Founded 1964. Left-wing political and literary weekly. Circulation 424,000.

10–12 place de la Bourse, 75081 Paris. Tel: (0)1 40-28-34-34. Fax: (0)1 42-36-19-63.

Le Canard Enchaîné

Founded 1915. Political satire weekly. Circulation 520,000.

173 rue Saint Honoré, 75051 Paris. Tel: (0)1 42-60-31-36. Fax: (0)1 42-27-97-87.

Periodicals

Paris-Match

Founded 1949. French and world affairs illustrated weekly. Circulation 690,000.

63 avenue des Champs Elysées, 75008 Paris.

Tel: (0)1 40-74-70-00. Fax: (0)1 40-74-76-35.

Web: www.parismatch.tm.fr

Book Publishers

Editions Arthaud SA

Founded 1890. Imprint of Flammarion SA. Subjects include art, history, literature, essays, sport and travel.

26 rue Racine, 75278 Paris. Tel: (0)1 40-51-31-00. Fax: (0)1 43-29-21-48.

Editions Bordas

Founded 1946. Subjects include education and general non-fiction.

21 rue du Montparnasse, 75283 Paris. Tel: (0)1 44-39-44-00. Fax: (0)1 44-39-41-07.

Editions Calmann-Lévy SA

Founded 1836. Subjects include fiction, biography, history, philosophy, psychology, sociology and economics.

3 rue Auber, 75009 Paris. Tel: (0)1 47-42-38-33.
Fax: (0)1 47-42-77-81.

Librairie Arthème Fayard

Founded 1854. Subjects include fiction, biography, history, philosophy, religion, sociology, general science and technology.

75 rue des Saints-Pères, 75278 Paris. Tel: (0)1 45-49-82-00.
Fax: (0)1 42-22-40-17.

Flammarion SA

Founded 1875. Subjects include fiction, literature, essays, art and general non-fiction.

26 rue Racine, 75278 Paris. Tel: (0)1 40-51-31-00.
Fax: (0)1 43-29-21-48.

Editions Gallimard

Founded 1911. Subjects include fiction, poetry, art, biography, history, philosophy and music.

5 rue Sébastien-Bottin, 75007 Paris. Tel: (0)1 40-54-14-57.
Fax: (0)1 49-54-14-51.

Hachette Groupe Livre

Founded 1826. Subjects include fiction and general non-fiction.

43 quai de Grenelle, 75905 Paris. Tel: (0)1 43-92-30-00.
Fax: (0)1 43-92-30-30.

Librairie Larousse

Founded 1852. Subjects include general and social sciences, technology, language, arts and linguistics.

17 rue du Montparnasse, 75298 Paris. Tel: (0)1 44-39-44-00.
Fax: (0)1 44-39-41-07.

Editions du Seuil

Founded 1935. Subjects include fiction, literature, essays, poetry, art, biography, history, philosophy, psychology, religion, general science and social sciences.

27 rue Jacob, 75261 Paris. Tel: (0)1 40-46-50-50.
Fax: (0)1 43-29-08-29.

Librairie Vuibert

Founded 1877. Subjects include biological and earth sciences,
chemistry, economics, law, mathematics and physics.

20 rue Berbier-du-Mets, 75013 Paris. Tel: (0)1 66-08-69-00.
Fax: (0)1 66-08-69-29.

TOURISM

There were 62,406,000 foreign tourists in 1996, spending
US$28·36bn. France receives more foreign tourists than any other
country, and had receipts in 1996 exceeded only in the USA and Italy.
Around 11m. foreigners a year visit Paris. Countries of origin (visitors,
in 1,000) in 1993: Germany, 12,900; UK, 8,000; Netherlands, 7,100;
Italy, 6,300; Spain, 3,000; Belgium, 2,000; USA, 1,900; Switzerland,
1,900; Portugal, 1,700; Sweden, 878; Canada, 694; Denmark, 687;
Ireland, 475; Greece, 348; Austria, 329; Japan, 320; Norway, 320.
There were 596,670 classified hotel rooms in 1994.

French Tourist Offices in the United Kingdom and the United States of America

UK

French Government Tourist Office, 178 Piccadilly, London, W1V 0AL.
Tel: (0)891 244123. Fax: (0)20 7493-6594.
E-mail: piccadilly@mdlf.demon.co.uk Web: www.franceguide.com

USA

French Government Tourist Office (New York), 444 Madison Ave.,
New York NY 10022. Tel: 212 838-7800. Fax: 212 838-7855.
E-mail: pubinfo@fgtousa.org

French Government Tourist Office (Illinois), 676 N. Michigan Ave., 3360 Chicago, IL 60611. Tel: 312 751-7800. Fax: 312 337-6339.

French Government Tourist Office (Texas), 2305 Cedar Springs Rd, Dallas, TX 75201. Tel: 214 720-4010. Fax: 214 720-0250.

French Government Tourist Office (California), 9454 Wilshire Blvd, 715 Beverly Hills, CA 90212-2967. Tel: 310 271-6665. Fax: 310 276-2835.

SPORT

The most famous French sport is cycling. The Tour de France is the world's most prestigious bicycle race. For three weeks every July, 189 of the world's top cyclists (in 21 teams of 9) race over 3,000 km roads through France. As well as all kinds of countryside conditions, the course includes the Alps and the Pyrenees, ending up on the Champs-Elysées in Paris. The local people line the route and wherever the race goes, normal life grinds to a halt. France is also football mad and the country hosted – and won – the 1998 world cup. The French team's home matches, friendlies and qualifiers for the 2000 World Cup are held in the Stade de France at Saint-Denis which was built for the World Cup. Rugby union has a strong following – mostly in the south and southwest of the country – and France takes part in the Five Nations Tournament (with England, Wales, Scotland and Ireland and – from 2000 – Italy). In tennis, the French Open is held in early June and is the second of the Gland Slam tournaments. Of the traditional sports, pétanque and the similar boules are still played on greens and hard surfaces in village and town squares all over France. Pelote, a fast ball game played with a racket, is played in the Basque country. In winter, French ski resorts attract millions of annual visitors. Information about sports can be found at any tourist office or from:

Minstère de la Jeunesse et des Sports, Direction des Sports
78 rue Olivier de Serres, 75739 Paris. Tel: (0)1 40-45-90-00.

Bureau de la Communication du Ministère: Tel: (0)1 40-45-92-07.

TRAVELLERS INFORMATION

Information Websites
Web: www.tourisme.fr www. franceguide.com www.paris.org
www.france.com www.w3i.com

Central Hotel Reservation Information
Central reservation numbers for hotel chains represented in the
UK with more than 100 hotels in France:
Best Western: 0800 39 31 30. Web: www.bestwestern.com
Choice Hotels: 0800 444 444. Web: www.choicehotelseurope.com
Châteaux et Hotels Independent: (0)20 7402-8182.
Ibis: (0)20 8283-4500. Web: www.accordhotel.com
Mercure: (0)20 8283-4500. Web: www.accordhotel.com
Novotel: (0)20 8283-4500. Web: www.accordhotel.com
Inter Hotel: (0)20 7287-3171.
Logis de France: (0)20 7287-3171.

Hotel Chains
Hilton International: 0345 581 595. Web. www.hilton.com
Holiday Inn: 0800 897 121. Web: basshotels.com

See also
Web: www.tourisme.fr www.franceguide.com www.paris.org
www.france.com www.w3i.com

Central Car Hire Reservation Information

Avis: Web: www.avis.com Tel: (0)1 46-10-60-60.

Hertz: Web: www.hertz.com Tel: (0)1 39-38-38-38/0803 861861.

Budget: Web: www.budgetrentacar.com Tel: 0800 181 181/
0541 565656.

Thrifty: Web: www.thrifty.com Tel: 0990 168238 (UK number).

Europcar: Web: www.europcar.com Tel: 0803 506506.

FESTIVALS AND MILLENNIUM EVENTS

Millennium Events

The French Government has launched a three-pronged plan to co-operate with numerous partners – communities, cultural institutions, government bodies, etc. – covering the period from autumn 1999 to April 2000 and create ways to celebrate the new Millennium.

A Time for Festivities: Focuses on 3 main celebrations; New Year's Eve (31 Dec. 1999), the annual music festival (21 June 2000) and Bastille Day (14 July 2000). The emphasis will be on 'doing away with borders' and new ways of being and living together. At regional level, there will be a Neighbourhood Festival (Marseilles), Colours of the World (Amiens) and Casa Musicale (Perpignan). There will be touring events such as Hip-Hop Caravan (the best of new and urban music on tour) and Children's Village, a travelling community of musicians from all over the world touring around meeting groups of children all over France.

A Time for Reflection: Forums of the year 2000 will invite the public to discuss issues that will affect them during the next millennium. The first was held in Lyon in Oct. 1997 and the last (to discuss 'France's Identity') will be held in Paris in May 2000. These discussions will culminate in the 'University of World Knowledge'. 365 seminars will be conducted by academics and researchers from all over the world in 3 Paris institutions – all open to the general public – and the result will be published as a 'Living Encyclopaedia of the Present Day'. There will also be 3 major exhibitions – Portraits of France (Paris), the French Language (Lyon) and Beauty (Avignon).

A Time for Creation: Will involve French and foreign artists in the performing and visual arts, architecture and urban design. So far, projects include The Children's Pavilion, the illumination of the Pont du Gard, The Life of Jesus (a photographic study) and a landscape project on the Island of Réunion.

Other projects include the creation of 'La Méridienne Verte' (the Green Meridian) – a line of trees running through France from north to south along the line of the Paris meridian. This will extend 1,200 km, cross 337 districts in 8 regions of France and cost 40m. francs. By June 2000 a footpath is also planned to run alongside the Green Meridian and on 14 July 2000 everyone will be invited to take part in a picnic along the line with an aerial flypast featuring all kinds of aircraft from balloons to Concorde. There is to be a new scientific theme park built in the Auvergne – Vulcania – a brainchild of former president Giscard d'Estaing. The major part of the park will be buried underground to minimize the impact on the surrounding volcanic landscape.

Avignon will be one of the 9 European Cities of Culture 2000.

Information: Mission for the Celebration of the Year 2000, 8 avenue de l'Opéra, 75001 Paris.
Tel: (0)1 55-04-20-00. Fax: (0)1 55-04-20-01.
Email: etudes@celebration2000.gouv.fr
Web: www.celebration2000.gouv.fr
Mission Avignon 2000: 9 rue Rempart de l'Oule, 84000 Avignon.
Tel: (0)4 90-86-17-65. Fax: (0)4 90-86-92-49.
Email: avignon.2000@wanadoo.fr

General information: www.franceguide.com www.tourism.fr

Annual Festivals

Early Feb.	Festival International du Court Metrage (Festival of short films)	Clermont-Ferrand
Late Feb.	Carnival (Mardi Gras)	Nice, Nantes
Late April	Festival du Film Court (short film festival)	Lille
May	Festival International du Film	Cannes
June	Eté Musical	Dijon
June	Festival International de Musique	Strasbourg
Mid-June	Festival du Jazz	Strasbourg
Late June	La Villette Jazz festival	Paris
Late June	Festival International du Film	La Rochelle
June–Aug.	Estivade (dance, music, theatre)	Dijon
June–July	Festival International Montpelier Danse	Montpelier
Late June	Printemps des Comediens	Montpelier
Early July (1st Sat.)	Festival du Thon (Tuna)	St-Jean-de-Luz
Early July	Tombée de la Nuit (Music, Dance, Theatre)	Rennes
July (2nd week)	Feria du Cheval (Festival of the Horse)	Stes-Marie-de-la-Mer
July	International Music Festival	Aix-en-Provence
July	Festival d'Anjou (Theatre)	Angers
Mid-July	Festival du Jazz	Nice
Early Aug.	Festival du Vin d'Alsace (Wine)	Colmar
Mid-July–mid-Aug.	Festival Paris	Paris
July–Aug.	Flâneries Musicales d'Eté (Music)	Reims
Aug.	International Mime Festival	Périgueux
Early Sept.	Fête de la Vigne (Wine)	Dijon
Early Oct.	Fête des Vendages à Montmartre (Wine)	Paris
Mid-Oct.	Festival des Allumées (Music, Dance, Theatre)	Nantes

Nov.	Festival Européen du Cinema d'Art et d'Essai (Art and Experimental Cinema)	Strasbourg
Nov. (2nd week)	Herring and Scallop Fair	Dieppe
Late Nov.	Fête des Trois Continents (Developing World Film)	Nantes

For more information, Tourist Offices have a brochure named 'Festive France' or see the internet site. Web:

www.tourisme.fr

www.franceguide.com

www.paris.org

www.france.com

www.w3i.com

FESTIVALS AND PUBLIC HOLIDAYS

1 Jan.	New Years Day,
March/April	Easter,
1 May	Labour Day,
May	Whit Sunday,
8 May	Fête de la Victoire 1945 (WWII Victory Day),
14 July	Bastille Day,
15 Aug.	Assumption of the Blessed Virgin Mary,
1 Nov.	All Saints Day,
11 Nov.	Armistice Day,
25 Dec.	Christmas Day,
26 Dec.	2nd Day of Christmas (in Alsace Lorraine-only),
31 Dec.	New Year's Eve.

ETIQUETTE

Social

Manners in France are more formal than in Britain. When you meet someone it is polite to shake hands and greet them with 'Bonjour' and then their name or, if you don't know it, 'Monsieur' or 'Madame'. 'Mademoiselle' should only be used to a young girl. The French do not use first names easily. When you know someone better they may kiss you on both cheeks. This is quite a formal greeting; kissing on one cheek is much more familiar so don't leave out the other side unless you are on intimate terms. When speaking French, it is polite to use the second person plural ('vous') not the more familiar second person singular ('tu') except to children, people you know very well or who have invited you to be more familiar, and animals. It is always worth trying to speak French – the effort will be appreciated even if you are responded to in English. Food and wine are a very important part of hospitality to the French so if you are invited to a meal in a private home express particular appreciation for the meal.

Tipping is widespread and even the attendants in restaurant and café cloakrooms and theatre ushers expect a tip.

Business

French business people are also very formal and French companies operate under very strict hierarchical rules. The managing director (or equivalent) is absolute boss, and so on down the line so that each level of management has a formal relationship with the one below. Appointments are not usually made before 9:30 in the morning although the working day may continue until well after 5:30 p.m. A verbal agreement is a preliminary to a written agreement. Only a written contract is legally binding. Letter writing in France is still extremely formal with elaborate forms of expression and it is almost impossible for a foreigner to negotiate the minefield of nuances, greetings, salutations and endings. It may be better to write business letters in English. It is polite to shake hands with everyone at the meeting and greet them by name, with their title if possible (e.g.: 'Monsieur le Directeur', etc.) or at least Monsieur or Madame. Smart dress is expected – suit and tie – and although increasing numbers of young people speak English, make an effort to start out the meeting in French.

DIPLOMATIC REPRESENTATIVES

Of France in Great Britain (58 Knightsbridge, London, SW1X 7JT)
Ambassador: Daniel Bernard.
Of Great Britain in France (35 rue du Faubourg St Honoré, 75383 Paris Cedex 08)
Ambassador: Sir Michael Jay, KCMG
Of France in the USA (4101 Reservoir Rd., NW, Washington, D.C., 20007)
Ambassador: François Bujon.
Of the USA in France (2 avenue Gabriel, Paris)
Ambassador: Felix Rohatyn.
Of France to the United Nations
Ambassador: Alain Dejammet.

Foreign Embassies
Australia: 4 rue Jean Rey, 75015 Paris. Tel: (0)1 40-59-33-00
Austria: 6 rue Fabert, 75007 Paris. Tel: (0)1 40-63-30-63
Belgium: 9 rue de Tilsitt, 75017 Paris. Tel: (0)1 44-09-39-39
Canada: 35 avenue Montaigne, 75008 Paris. Tel: (0)1 44-43-29-00
China (People's Republic): 11 avenue George V, 75008 Paris.
Tel: (0)1 47-23-34-45

Denmark: 77 avenue Marceau, 75116 Paris. Tel: (0)1 44-31-21-21

Germany: 13–15 avenue Franklin D. Roosevelt, 75008 Paris.

Tel: (0)1 53-83-45-00

Greece: 17 rue Auguste Vacquerie, 75116 Paris. Tel: (0)1 47-23-72-28

Holy See: 10 avenue du Président Wilson, 75116 Paris.

Tel: (0)1 47-23-58-34

Ireland: 12 avenue Foch, 75116 Paris. Tel: (0)1 44-17-67-00

Italy: 51 rue de Varenne, 75007 Paris. Tel: (0)1 45-44-38-90

Japan: 7 avenue Hoche, 75008 Paris. Tel: (0)1 48-88-62-00

Luxembourg: 33 avenue Rapp, 75007 Paris. Tel: (0)1 45- 55-13-37

Netherlands: 7–9 rue Elbé, 75007 Paris. Tel: (0)1 43-06-61-88

New Zealand: 7 ter, rue Léonard de Vinci, 75116 Paris.

Tel: (0)1 45-00-24-11

Norway: 28 rue Bayard, 75008 Paris. Tel: (0)1 53-67-04-00

Portugal: 3 rue de Noisiel, 75116 Paris. Tel: (0)1 47-27-35-29

Russia: 40 boulevard Lannes, 75116 Paris. Tel: (0)1 45-04-05-50

South Africa: 59 quai d'Orsay, 75343 Paris. Tel: (0)1 45-55-92-37

Spain: 22 avenue Marceau, 75008 Paris. Tel: (0)1 44-43-18-00

Sweden: 17 rue Barbet de Jouy, 75007 Paris. Tel: (0)1 44-18-88-00

Switzerland: 142 rue de Grenelle, 75007 Paris. Tel: (0)1 49-55-67-00

Turkey: 16 avenue de Lamballe, 75116 Paris. Tel: (0)1 45-24-52-24

United Kingdom: 35 rue du Faubourg Saint Honoré, 75383 Paris.

Tel: (0)1 44-51-31-00

USA: 2 avenue Gabriel, 75382 Paris. Tel: (0)1 43-12-22-22

FURTHER READING

Institut National de la Statistique et des Études Économiques: *Annuaire statistique de la France* (from 1878); *Bulletin mensuel de statistique* (monthly); *Documentation économique* (bi-monthly); *Economie et*

Statistique (monthly); *Tableaux de l'Économie Française* (biennially, from 1956); *Tendances de la Conjoncture* (monthly).

Ardagh, J., *France in the New Century*. Viking, London, 1999

Ardant, P., *Les Institutions de la Vie République*. Paris, 1992

Balladur, E., *Deux Ans à Matignon*. Paris, 1995

Braudel, F., *The Identity of France*. 2 vols. London, 1988-90

Caron, F., *An Economic History of Modern France*. London, 1979

Chafer, Tony and Sackur, Amanda, (eds) *French Colonial Empire and the Popular Front*. Macmillan, 1999

Chambers, F. J., *France*. [Bibliography] ABC-Clio, Oxford and Santa Barbara (CA), (rev. ed.) 1990

Chambers, F. J., *Paris*. [Bibliography] ABC-Clio, Oxford and Santa Barbara (CA), 1998

Chazal, C., *Balladur*. [in French] Paris, 1993

Cubertafond, A., *Le Pouvoir, la Politique et l'État en France*. Paris, 1993

L'État de la France. Paris, annual

Gildea, R., *France since 1945*. Oxford University Press, 1996

Gouze, R., *Mitterrand par Mitterrand*. Paris, 1994

Hollifield, J. F. and Ross, G., *Searching for the New France*. Routledge, London, 1991

Hudson, G. L., *Corsica*. [World Bibliographic Series, vol. 202] ABC-Clio, Oxford, 1997

Jack, A., *The French Exception*. Profile Books, London, 1999

Jones, C., *The Cambridge Illustrated History of France*. Cambridge University Press, 1994

McMillan, J. F., *Twentieth-Century France: Politics and Society in France, 1898–1991*. 2nd ed. [of *Dreyfus to De Gaulle*]. Arnold, London, 1992

Mendras, H. and Cole, A., *Social Change in Modern France: towards a Cultural Anthropology of the Fifth Republic*. Cambridge University Press, 1991

Menon, Anand, *France, NATO and the Limits of Independence, 1981-97*. Macmillan, 1999

Morris, P., *French Politics Today.* Manchester University Press, 1994

Noin, D. and White, P. *Paris.* John Wiley, Chichester, 1997

Pinchemel, P., *France: A Geographical, Social and Economic Survey.* Cambridge University Press, 1987

Popkin, J. D., *A History of Modern France.* New York, 1994

Price, R., *Concise History of France.* Cambridge University Press, 1993

Raymond, Gino G., (ed.) *Structures of Power in Modern France.* Macmillan, 1999

Schmidt, V. A., *Democratizing France: the Political and Administrative History of Decentralization.* Cambridge University Press, 1991

Stevens, A., *The Government and Politics of France.* Macmillan, London, 1992

Tiersky, Ronald, *Mitterrand in Light and Shadow.* Macmillan, 1999

Agulhon, M. and Nevill, A., *The French Republic, 1879–1992.* Blackwell, Oxford, 1993

Tippett-Spiritou, Sandy, *French Catholicism.* Macmillan, 1999

Todd, E., *The Making of Modern France: Politics, Ideology and Culture.* Oxford, 1991

Verdié, M. (ed.) *L'État de la France et de ses Habitants.* Paris, 1992

Vesperini, J.-P., *L'Économie de la France sous la Ve République.* Paris, 1993

Zeldin, T., *The French.* Harvill Press, London, 1997

Who's Who in France [in French]. Paris, annual

(Also see specialized titles listed under relevant selections, above.)

National statistical office: Institut National de la Statistique et des Etudes Économiques (INSEE), 75582 Paris Cedex 12.

Website: //www.insee.fr/

Tourist and Hotel Guides

Baillie, K. and Salmon, T., *France: the Rough Guide.* Rough Guides, 1999.

Eyewitness Travel Guide to France. Dorling Kindersley, 1994.

Fodor's 99 France (Fodor's Gold Guides). Fodor's Travel Publications, 1998.

Hotels in France 1999. AA Publishing.

Johansens Recommended Hotels: Europe and the Mediterranean 2000. Johansen.

Let's Go 1999: France. Macmillan.

Robinson, D., *The Simple Guide to France, Customs and Etiquette.* Global Books, 1998.

Lonely Planet: Corsica. Lonely Planet Publications, 1999.

Lonely Planet: France. Lonely Planet Publications, 1999.

Michelin Red Guide Europe 1999: Hotels–Restaurants. Michelin.

Michelin Green Guide: France. Michelin, 1996.

Michelin Red Guide: France. Michelin, 1999.

DEPARTMENTS AND TERRITORIES OVERSEAS

These fall into 3 categories: *Overseas Departments* (French Guiana, Guadeloupe, Martinique, Réunion); *Territorial Collectivities* (Mayotte, St Pierre and Miquelon); and *Overseas Territories* (French Polynesia, New Caledonia, Southern and Antarctic Territories, Wallis and Futuna).

FURTHER READING

Aldrich, R. and Connell, J., *France's Overseas Frontier: Départements et Territoires d'Outre-Mer.* Cambridge University Press, 1992

Overseas Departments

Guadeloupe

Key Historical Events

The islands were discovered by Columbus in 1493. The Carib inhabitants resisted Spanish attempts to colonize. A French colony was established on 28 June 1635, and apart from short periods of occupancy by British forces, Guadeloupe has since remained a French possession. On 19 March 1946 Guadeloupe became an Overseas Department.

Territory and Population

Guadeloupe consists of a group of islands in the Lesser Antilles. The two main islands, Basse-Terre (to the west) and Grande-Terre (to the east), are joined by a bridge over a narrow channel. Adjacent to these are the islands of Marie Galante (to the south-east), La Désirade (to the east), and the Îles des Saintes (to the south); the islands of St Martin and St Barthélemy lie 250 km to the north-west.

Island	Area (sq. km)	1990 Census	Chief town
St Martin[1]	54[2]	28,518	Marigot
St Barthélemy	21	5,038	Gustavia
Basse-Terre	848	149,943	Basse-Terre
Grande-Terre	590	177,570	Pointe-à-Pitre
Îles des Saintes	13	2,036	Terre-de-Bas
La Désirade	20	1,610	Grande Anse
Marie-Galante	158	13,463	Grand-Bourg
	1,705	378,178[3]	

[1] Northern part only; the southern third is Dutch.

[2] Includes uninhabited Tintamarre.

[3] Preliminary results.

Population at the last census (1990, final result), 386,987; 1995 estimate, 417,000. The projected population for 2000 is 425,000. An estimated 99·4% of the population were urban in 1995. Population of principal towns: Basse-Terre, 14,082; Pointe-à-Pitre, 26,031; Les Abymes, 62,645. Basse-Terre is the seat of government, while larger Pointe-à-Pitre is the department's main economic centre and port; Les Abymes is a 'suburb' of Pointe-à-Pitre.

French is the official language, but Creole is spoken by the vast majority, except on St Martin.

Social Statistics
1998 estimates (per 1,000 population): birth rate, 16·7; death rate, 5·6. Annual growth rate, 1990–95, 2·1%. Life expectancy at birth, 1990–95, 71·1 years for males and 78·0 years for females.

Climate
Warm and humid. Pointe-à-Pitre, Jan. 74°F (23·4°C), July 80°F (26·7°C). Annual rainfall 71" (1,814 mm).

Constitution and Government

Guadeloupe is administered by a General Council of 42 members directly elected for 6-year terms (assisted by an Economic and Social Committee of 40 members) and by a Regional Council of 41 members. It is represented in the National Assembly by 4 deputies; in the Senate by 2 senators; and on the Economic and Social Council by 1 councillor. There are 4 *arrondissements,* sub-divided into 42 cantons and 34 communes, each administered by an elected municipal council. The French government is represented by an appointed Prefect.

Current Administration

Prefect: Michel Diefenbacher.
President of the General Council: Dominique Larifla (DVG).
President of the Regional Council: Lucette Michaux-Chevry (RPR).

Economy

Performance

In 1993 the GDP was 18,984m. French francs. GDP per capita (1993) was 46,484 French francs. Real GDP growth was −2·9% in 1995 and 1·9% in 1994.

Currency

The French franc is in use.

Banking and Finance

The Caisse Française de Développement is the official bank of the department, and issues its bank-notes. The main commercial banks in 1995 (with number of branches) were: Banque des Antilles Françaises (6), Banque Régionale d'Escompte et de Depôts (5), Banque Nationale de Paris (8), Crédit Agricole (18), Banque Française Commerciale (8), Société Générale de Banque aux Antilles (5), Credit Lyonnais (6), Credit Martiniquais (3), Banque Inschauspé et Cie (1).

Energy and Natural Resources

Electricity

Total production (1994): 1,005m. kWh.

Agriculture

Chief products (1993): bananas, 105,400 tonnes; sugar-cane, 748,000 tonnes; flowers, 8·9m. (1992). Other fruits and vegetables are also grown for both export and domestic consumption.

Livestock (1996): Cattle, 60,000; goats, 63,000 (1995); sheep, 3,000; pigs, 14,000.

Forestry

In 1995 forests covered 89,000 ha, or 47·3% of the total land area (down from 51·5% in 1990). Timber production in 1995 was 15,000 cu. metres.

Fisheries

Total catches in 1995 were 9,530 tonnes, almost exclusively from sea fishing.

Industry

The main industries are sugar refining, food processing and rum distilling, carried out by small and medium-sized businesses. Other important industries are cement production and tourism.

Labour

The economically active population in 1997 was approximately 128,000. In 1993 there were 15,020 persons in the trade sector; 6,950 in transport and communications; and 34,223 in services. The minimum wage (SMIC) was 39·29 francs per hour (6,664 a month) in 1997. 46,360 persons were registered unemployed in 1994.

International Trade
Imports and Exports
Total imports (1995): US$1,890m.; total exports: US$159m. Main export products (1993, with % of market share): bananas, 26%; sugar, 26%, rum, 7%. Trade with France (1993): 68% of all imports; 78% of exports.

Communications
Roads
In 1996 there were 3,200 km of roads. In 1993 there were 101,600 passenger cars and 37,500 commercial vehicles.

Civil Aviation
Air France and a dozen or so other airlines call at Guadeloupe airport. In 1996 there were 38,243 arrivals and departures of aircraft, and 1,688,252 passengers at Le Raizet (Pointe-à-Pitre) airport. There are also airports at Marie-Galante, La Désirade, St Barthélemy and St Martin. Most domestic services are operated by Société Nouvelle Air Guadeloupe.

Shipping
In 1993, 2,812 vessels arrived to disembark 105,217 passengers and 1,933,000 tonnes of freight; and to embark 95,882 passengers and 431,000 tonnes of freight.

Telecommunications
In 1996 there were 170,700 main telephone lines, and in 1995, 3,400 fax machines.

Postal Services
In 1984 there were 47 post offices.

Social Institutions

Justice

There are 4 *tribunaux d'instance* and 2 *tribunaux de grande instance* at Basse-Terre and Pointe-à-Pitre; there is also a court of appeal and a court of assizes.

Religion

The majority of the population are Roman Catholic.

Education

Education is free and compulsory from 6 to 16 years. In 1994 there were 54,493 pupils at 321 pre-elementary and primary schools, and 46,176 at 20 *lycées* and 40 *collèges* at secondary level. In 1993 there were 4,308 students from Guadeloupe at the University of Antilles-Guyana (out of total number of 8,290).

Health

In 1995 there were 13 public hospitals and 16 private clinics. In 1993 there were 590 doctors, 119 dentists, 1,470 nurses, 206 pharmacists and 108 midwives.

Culture

Broadcasting

Radiodiffusion Française d'Outre-Mer broadcasts for 17 hours a day in French. There is a local region radio station, and several private stations. There are 2 television channels (1 regional; 1 satellite) broadcasting for 6 hours a day. There were (1995) 98,000 radio and 114,000 TV receivers.

Press

There was (1995) 1 daily newspaper with a circulation of 20,000.

Tourism

Tourism is the chief economic activity. 458,181 tourists visited in 1994, including 313,613 cruise visitors.

French Guiana

Key Historical Events

A French settlement on the island of Cayenne was established in 1604 and the territory between the Maroni and Oyapock rivers finally became a French possession in 1817. Convict settlements were established from 1852, that on Devil's Island being the most notorious; all were closed by 1945. On 19 March 1946 the status of French Guiana was changed to that of an Overseas Department.

Territory and Population

French Guiana is situated on the north-east coast of Latin America, and is bounded in the north-east by the Atlantic Ocean, west by Suriname, and south and east by Brazil. It includes the offshore Devil's Island, Royal Island and St Joseph, and has an area of 85,534 sq. km. Population at the 1990 census: 114,808 (including 34,087 of foreign origin); estimate (1995), 150,000. The projected population for 2000 is 173,000. In 1995, 76·4% lived in urban areas. The chief towns are: the capital, Cayenne (41,600 inhabitants), Kourou (14,000) and Saint-Laurent-du-Maroni (13,900). About 58% of inhabitants are of African descent. The official language is French.

Social Statistics

1998 estimates (per 1,000 population): Birth rate, 23·7; death rate, 4·5. 49% of the poplation are migrants. Annual growth rate, 1990–95, 4·6%.

Climate

Equatorial type climate with most of the country having a main rainy season between April and July and a fairly dry period between August and Dec. Both temperatures and humidity are high the whole year round. Cayenne, Jan. 26°C, July 29°C. Annual rainfall 3,202 mm.

Constitution and Government

French Guiana is administered by a General Council of 19 members directly elected for 5-year terms, and by a Regional Council of 31 members. It is represented in the National Assembly by 2 deputies; in the Senate by 1 senator. The French government is represented by a Prefect. There are 2 *arrondissements* (Cayenne and Saint Laurent-du-Maroni) sub-divided into 22 communes and 19 cantons.

Current Administration

Prefect: Pierre Dartout.
President of the General Council: Stéphan Phinera (PS).
President of the Regional Council: Antoine Karam (PS).

Economy

Performance

In 1993 the GDP was 7,989m. French francs. GDP per capita (1993) was 54,516 French francs. Real GDP growth was 20·9% in both 1994 and 1995.

Currency

The French franc is in use.

Banking and Finance

The Caisse Centrale de Coopération Economique is the bank of issue. In 1995 commercial banks included the Banque Nationale de Paris-Guyane, Crédit Populaire Guyanais and Banque Française Commerciale.

Energy and Natural Resources

Electricity

Installed capacity was 228,000 kW in 1995. Production in 1994 was 446m. kWh.

Minerals

Placer gold mining is the most important industry in French Guiana. In 1993, 2,795 kg of gold were produced.

Agriculture

Some 21,670 ha are estimated to be under cultivation. Principal crops (1993, in tonnes): rice, 26,962; manioc, 23,350; sugar-cane, 3,200.

Livestock (1996): 8,000 cattle; 9,000 pigs; 3,000 sheep; 220,000 poultry (1993).

Forestry

The country has immense forests which are rich in many kinds of timber. In 1995 forests covered 79,900 sq. km, or 90·6% of the total land area. 90·7% had been under forests in 1990. Roundwood production (1995) 132,000 cu. metres. The trees also yield oils, essences and gum products.

Fisheries

The catch in 1995 was 7,737 tonnes. Shrimps account for nearly 45% of the total catch.

Industry

Important products include rum, rosewood essence and beer. The island has sawmills and 1 sugar factory.

Labour

The economically active population (1993) was 46,300. In 1997 the minimum wage (SMIC) was 39·29 francs per hour (6,664 francs a month). 8,324 persons were registered unemployed in 1994.

International Trade

Imports and Exports

Total trade (1995); imports, US$752m.; exports, US$131m.

Communications

Roads

There were (1996) 356 km of national and 366 km of departmental roads. In 1993 there were 29,100 passenger cars and 10,600 commercial vehicles.

Civil Aviation

In 1996 Rochambeau International Airport (Cayenne) handled 362,756 passengers and 5,460 tonnes of freight. Services were provided in 1998 by Air France, AOM, Société Nouvelle Air Guadeloupe and Surinam Airways. The base of the European Space Agency (ESA) is located near Kourou and has been operational since 1979.

Shipping

359 vessels arrived and departed in 1993; 249,160 tonnes of petroleum products and 230,179 tonnes of other products were discharged, and 69,185 tonnes of freight loaded. Chief ports: Cayenne, St-Laurent-du-Maroni and Kourou. There are also inland waterways navigable by small craft.

Telecommunications

The number of telephone main lines in 1997 was 46,700 (298·5 per 1,000 population).

Social Institutions

Justice

At Cayenne there is a *tribunal d'instance* and a *tribunal de grande instance*, from which appeal is to the regional *cour d'appel* in Martinique.

Religion

In 1997 approximately 52% of the population was Roman Catholic.

Education

Primary education is free and compulsory. There were 24,000 children at primary schools in 1993; 12,000 at secondary schools; and (1988) a further 2,224 registered at private schools. In 1993, 644 students from French Guiana attended the Henri Visioz Institute, which forms part of the University of Antilles-Guyana (8,290 students in 1993).

Health

In 1995 there were 2 hospitals with 567 beds, 3 private clinics and a care centre. There were (1994) 213 doctors, 38 dentists, 47 pharmacists, 40 midwives and 495 nursing personnel.

Culture

Broadcasting

Radiodiffusion Française d'Outre-Mer-Guyane broadcasts for 133 hours each week on medium- and short-waves, and FM in French. Television is broadcast for 60 hours each week on 2 channels. In 1995 there were 95,000 radio and 26,000 TV receivers; colour is by SECAM. Although the number of televisions went up between 1980 and 1995, there were only 181 televisions per 1,000 inhabitants in 1995, down from 191 per 1,000 in 1980. Nowhere else in the world did the rate come down over the same 15-year period – in general access to television has become more widespread.

Press

There was (1996) 1 daily newspaper with a circulation of 1,000, and a second paper published 4 times a week has a circulation of 5,500.

Tourism

Total number of visitors (1993), 54,000.

FURTHER READING

Crane, Janet, *French Guiana* [Bibliography]. ABC-Clio, Oxford and Santa Barbara (CA), 1998

Martinique

Key Historical Events

Discovered by Columbus in 1502, Martinique became a French colony in 1635, and apart from brief periods of British occupation the island has since remained under French control. On 19 March 1946 its status was altered to that of an Overseas Department.

Territory and Population

The island, situated in the Lesser Antilles between Dominica and St Lucia, occupies an area of 1,128 sq. km. Population at last census (1990), 359,572; estimate (1995), 383,621; density, 357 per sq. km. The projected population for 2000 is 416,000. An estimated 93·3% of the population were urban in 1995. Population of principal towns: the capital and main port Fort-de-France, 101,540; Le Lamentin, 30,026; Schoelcher, 19,825; Sainte-Marie, 19,683; Rivière-Pilote, 11,261; La Trinité, 10,330. French is the official language but the majority of people speak Creole.

Social Statistics

1998 estimates per 1,000 population: birth rate, 16·5; death rate, 5·9. Annual growth rate, 1990–95, 0·9%. Life expectancy at birth, 1990–95, 73·0 years for males and 79·5 years for females.

Climate

The dry season is from Dec. to May, and the humid season from June to Nov. Fort-de-France, Jan. 74°F (23·5°C), July 78°F (25·6°C). Annual rainfall 72" (1,840 mm).

Constitution and Government

The island is administered by a *General Council* of 45 members directly elected for 6-year terms, and by a Regional Council of 42

members. The French government is represented by an appointed
Prefect. There are 4 *arrondissements*, sub-divided into 45 cantons and
34 communes, each administered by an elected municipal council.
Martinique is represented in the National Assembly by 4 deputies, in
the Senate by 2 senators and on the Economic and Social Council by
1 councillor.

Current Administration

Prefect: Jean-François Cordet.
President of the General Council: Claude Lise (PPM).
President of the Regional Council: Emile Capgras (PCM).

Economy

Main sectors of activity: tradeable services, distribution, industry,
building and public works, transport and telecommunications,
agriculture and tourism.

Performance

In 1993 the GDP was FF22,969m. GDP per capita was FF60,861.
Real GDP growth was –2·9% in 1995 and 1·9% in 1994.

Banking and Finance

The Institut d'Émission des Départements d'Outre-Mer is the official
bank. The Caisse Centrale de Développement is the government's
vehicle for the promotion of economic development in the region. There
were 5 commercial banks, 4 co-operative banks, 1 savings bank, 5
investment companies and 2 specialized financial institutions in 1999.

Energy and Natural Resources

Electricity

A network of 4,084 km of cables supplies 134,331 customers.
Electricity is produced by 2 fuel-powered stations. Total production
(1994): 903m. kWh.

Agriculture

Chief products: bananas, rum, sugar, pineapples, food and vegetables. In 1993 there were 3,223 ha under sugar-cane, 8,500 ha under bananas and 600 ha under pineapples. Production (1993 in tonnes): sugar, 6,626; sugar-cane, 227,076; bananas (1992), 228,000; pineapples (1992), 28,500.

Livestock (1996): 30,000 cattle, 42,000 sheep, 33,000 pigs, 23,000 goats (1995) and 263,000 poultry (1993).

Forestry

In 1995 there were 38,000 ha of forest, or 35·8% of the total land area (down from 37·7% in 1990). Timber production in 1995 was 12,000 cu. metres.

Fisheries

The catch in 1995 was 5,377 tonnes, almost exclusively from sea fishing.

Industry

Some food processing and chemical engineering is carried out by small and medium-size businesses. There were 9,443 businesses in 1993 (30% in building). There is an important cement industry; 12 distilleries for rum; and an oil refinery, with an annual treatment capacity of 0·75m. tonnes. Martinique has 5 industrial zones.

Labour

In 1995, 7·6% of the working population were in agriculture; 17·6% in industry; 23·8% in retail; 34·1% in services; 16·9% in distribution. In 1997 the minimum wage (SMIC) was FF6,663 a month (39·43 an hour). The economically active population in 1994 was 164,870. Some 61,100 persons were unemployed in 1995.

International Trade

Imports and Exports

Martinique has a structural trade deficit due to the nature of goods traded. It imports high-value-added goods (foodstuffs, capital goods, consumer goods and motor vehicles) and exports agricultural produce (bananas) and refined oil.

In 1995 imports were valued at US$1,963m.; exports at US$224m. Main trading partners: France, EU, French Guiana and Guadeloupe. Trade with France accounted for 63% of imports and 61% of exports in 1995.

Communications

Roads

Martinique has 2,176 km of roads. In 1995, FF106m. was spent on improving them. In 1993 there were 108,300 passenger cars and 32,200 commercial vehicles.

Rail

In 1995 there were 1,606 km of roads, of which 1,200 km were surfaced. 252 km were classified as national routes and 862 km as first-class roads. In 1992 there were 12,591 passenger cars and 2,443 commercial vehicles registered.

Civil Aviation

There is an international airport at Fort-de-France (Lamentin). In 1996 it handled 1,611,970 passengers and 13,738 tonnes of freight. 8 scheduled companies use Fort-de-France: Air France, Air Liberté, American Airlines, AOM, Air Calypso, Air Guadeloupe, Corsair and Liat.

Shipping

The island is visited regularly by French, American and other lines. The main sea links to and from Martinique are ensured by CGM Sud.

It links Martinique to Europe and some African and American companies. Since 1995 new scheduled links have been introduced between Martinique, French Guiana, Haiti and Panama. These new links will facilitate exchanges between Martinique, Latin America and the Caribbean, especially Cuba. In 1993, 2,856 vessels called at Martinique and discharged 80,605 passengers and 1,612,000 tonnes of freight, and embarked 82,119 passengers and 789,000 tonnes of freight.

Telecommunications
In 1997 there were 169,900 main telephone lines. There were (1995) 12,000 cellular phone subscribers, 20,000 fax machines and 36,000 PCs. The main operator is France Télécom.

Social Institutions
Justice
Justice is administered by 2 lower courts (*tribunaux d'instance*), a higher court (*tribunal de grande instance*), a regional court of appeal, a commercial court and an administrative court.

Religion
In 1997, 95% of the population was Roman Catholic.

Education
Education is compulsory between the ages of 6 and 16 years. In 1994 there were 51,824 pupils in 263 nursery and primary schools, and 43,384 pupils in 61 secondary schools. There were 29 institutes of higher education. In 1993, 3,670 students from Martinique were registered at the University of Antilles-Guyana (out of a total of 8,290).

Health
In 1995 there were 8 hospitals, 3 private clinics and 7 nursing homes. Total number of beds, 2,100. There were 680 doctors, 230 pharmacists, 123 dentists, 1,700 nurses, 147 midwives, 141 physiotherapists and 48 speech therapists.

Culture

Broadcasting

Radio Diffusion Française d'Outre-Mer broadcasts on FM wave, and operates 2 channels (1 satellite). There are also 2 commercial TV stations. In 1995 there were 77,000 radio and 55,000 TV receivers (colour by SECAM).

Press

In 1996 there was 1 daily newspaper with a circulation of 30,000.

Tourism

In 1996 there were 477,000 tourist arrivals by air. Receipts totalled US$392m. There are 122 hotels, with 4,460 rooms.

FURTHER READING

Crane, Janet, *Martinique* [Bibliography]. ABC-Clio, Oxford and Santa Barbara (CA), 1995

Réunion

Key Historical Events

Réunion (formerly Île Bourbon) became a French possession in 1638 and remained so until 19 March 1946, when its status was altered to that of an Overseas Department.

Territory and Population

The island of Réunion lies in the Indian Ocean, about 880 km east of Madagascar and 210 km south-west of Mauritius. It has an area of 2,504 sq. km. Population at the 1990 census: 597,828; 1996 estimate, 700,000, giving a density of 280 per sq. km; projection (2005), 900,000. An estimated 67·7% of the population were rural in 1995. The capital is Saint-Denis (population, 1995: 207,158); other large towns are Saint-Pierre (192,462), Saint-Paul (113,071) and le Tampon (47,593).

The islands of Juan de Nova, Europa, Bassas da India, Îles Glorieuses and Tromelin, with a combined area of 32 sq. km, are uninhabited and lie in the Indian Ocean adjacent to Madagascar. They remained French after Madagascar's independence in 1960, and are now administered by the Commissioner of Réunion. Both Mauritius and the Seychelles lay claim to Tromelin; and Madagascar claims all 5 islands.

French is the official language, but Creole is also spoken.

Social Statistics

1997: Live births, 13,748; deaths, 3,609; marriages, 3,284. Birth rate per 1,000 population (1994), 20·7; death rate, 5·3. Annual growth rate, 1990–95, 1·7%. Life expectancy at birth, 1990–95, 69·4 years for males and 78·8 years for females. Infant mortality, 1990–95, 8 per 1,000 live births; fertility rate, 2·4 births per woman.

Climate

There is a sub-tropical maritime climate, free from extremes of weather, although the island lies in the cyclone belt of the Indian Ocean. Conditions are generally humid and there is no well-defined dry season. Saint-Denis, Jan. 80°F (26·7°C), July 70°F (21·1°C). Annual rainfall 56" (1,400 mm).

Constitution and Government

Réunion is administered by a General Council of 48 members directly elected for 6-year terms, and by a Regional Council of 45 members. Réunion is represented in the National Assembly in Paris by 5 deputies; in the Senate by 3 senators; and in the Economic and Social Council by 1 councillor. There are 4 *arrondissements* sub-divided into 47 cantons and 24 communes, each administered by an elected municipal council. The French government is represented by an appointed Commissioner.

Current Administration

Prefect: Jean Daubigny.
President of the General Council: Jean-Luc Poudroux.
President of the Regional Council: Paul Verges.

Economy

Performance

GDP was FF35,266m. in 1994. Real GDP growth was 2·7% in 1995.
GDP per capita (1993) was FF52,946.

Currency

The French franc is in use.

Banking and Finance

The Institut d'Émission des Départements d'Outre-mer has the right
to issue bank-notes. Banks operating in Réunion are the Banque de la
Réunion (Crédit Lyonnais), the Banque Nationale de Paris
Intercontinentale, the Caisse Régionale de Crédit Agricole Mutuel de
la Réunion, the Banque Française Commerciale (BFC) CCP,
Trésorerie Générale, and the Banque de la Réunion pour l'Économie
et la Développement (BRED).

Energy and Natural Resources

Electricity

Production (1997), 1,470·8m. kWh. Consumption per capita (1994),
1,670 kWh.

Oil and Gas

Production (1997), 184,035 tonnes.

Water

Production (1997), 100·6m. cu metres.

Agriculture

Production of sugar was 207,110 tonnes in 1997; rum, 71,822 hectolitres (pure alcohol) in 1997. Other important products (1995, in tonnes): tobacco, 37; potatoes, 9; geranium oil, 5·3; onions, 2,415; pineapples (1996), 7·2; vanilla (1997), 48; maize (1992), 13,270.

Livestock (1997): 23,460 cattle, 87,170 pigs, 31,200 sheep, 11,835 poultry and 32,000 goats (1995). Meat production (1993, in tonnes): beef 1,206, pork 9,850 and poultry 14,080. Milk production (1997), 13,986 hectolitres.

Forestry

There were 89,000 ha of forest in 1995, or 35·6% of the total land area. Timber production in 1995 was 36,000 cu. metres.

Fisheries

In 1997 the catch was 5,882 tonnes, almost entirely from marine waters. Deep-sea fishing (1999) is mainly for blue marlin, sail-fish, blue-fin tuna and sea bream.

Industry

The major industries are electricity and sugar. Food processing, chemical engineering, printing and the production of perfume, textiles, leathers, tobacco, wood and construction materials are carried out by small and medium-sized businesses. At the beginning of 1994 there were 9,465 craft businesses employing about 20,000 persons.

Labour

The workforce was 264,200 in 1993. The minimum wage (SMIC) was 39·29 francs an hour (6,664 a month) in 1997. On 1 Jan. 1997, 96,330 persons were registered unemployed, a rate of 36·7%.

International Trade
Imports and Exports
Trade in 1m. French francs:

	1994	1995	1996	1997
Imports	13,070	13,494	14,214	14,262
Exports	954	1,036	1,071	1,250

The chief export is sugar, accounting for 57% of total exports (1994). In 1994, 67% of imports and 74% of exports were from and to France.

Communications
Roads
There were, in 1994, 2,724 km of roads. In Jan. 1998 there were 219,456 registered vehicles. In 1999 the County Council was operating bus services to all towns.

Civil Aviation
Réunion is served by Air Austral, Air France, AOM French Airlines, Air Liberté, Air Madagascar, Air Mauritius and Corsair. In 1997, 661,709 passengers and 13,640 tonnes of freight arrived at, and 658,292 passengers and 5,953 tonnes of freight departed from, Roland Garros Saint-Denis airport.

Shipping
604 vessels visited the island in 1997, unloading 2,301,800 tonnes of freight and loading 453,600 tonnes at Port-Réunion.

Telecommunications
The number of telephone main lines in 1997 was 236,500. In 1995 there were 1,900 fax machines.

Postal Services
In 1996 there were 824 post offices.

Social Institutions

Justice

There are 3 lower courts (*tribunaux d'instance*), 2 higher courts (*tribunaux de grande instance*), 1 appeal, 1 administrative court and 1 conciliation board.

Religion

In 1990, 95% of the population was Roman Catholic.

Education

In 1997–98 there were 351 primary schools with 120,190 pupils. Secondary education was provided in 26 *lycées,* 69 colleges, and 16 technical *lycées*, with, together, 94,072 pupils. The *Université Française de l'Océan Indien* (founded 1971) had 12,485 students in 1997–98.

Health

In 1997 there were 19 hospitals with 2,799 beds, 1,268 doctors, 305 dentists, 275 pharmacists, 184 midwives and 2,980 nursing personnel.

Culture

Broadcasting

Radiodiffusion Française d'Outre-Mer broadcasts in French on medium- and short-waves for more than 18 hours a day. There are 2 national television channels (*RFD1, Tempo*) and 3 independent channels (*Antenne Réunion, Canal Réunion/Canal +* and *TV Sud*). In 1995 there were 120,000 TV receivers and 165,000 radio receivers.

Cinema

In 1995 there were 17 cinemas.

Press

There were (1998) 3 daily newspapers (*Quotidien, Journal de l'Île, Témoignages*), 2 weekly (*Visu, Télé Magazine*), 3 monthly (*Memento,*

Via, l'Eco Austral) and 1 fortnightly magazine (*Leader*), with a combined circulation of 57,000.

Tourism

Tourism is a major resource industry. There were 370,255 visitors in 1997 (82% French). Receipts (1996) totalled US$258m. In 1999 there were 50 hotels, 94 country lodges (*gîtes ruraux*), 204 bed and breakfast houses, 19 stopover lodges (*gîtes d'étape*) and 9 country houses.

Libraries

There were 53 libraries in 1998.

FURTHER READING

Institut National de la Statistique et des Etudes Économiques: *Tableau Économique de la Réunion*. Paris (annual)

Bertile, W., *Atlas Thématique et Régional*. Réunion, 1990

Territorial Collectivities

Mayotte

Key Historical Events

Mayotte was a French colony from 1843 until 1914 when it was attached, with the other Comoro islands, to the government-general of Madagascar. The Comoro group was granted administrative autonomy within the French Republic and became an Overseas Territory. When the other 3 islands voted to become independent (as the Comoro state) in 1974, Mayotte voted against this and remained a French dependency. In Dec. 1976 it became (following a further referendum) a Territorial Collectivity.

Territory and Population

Mayotte, east of the Comoro Islands, consists of a main island (362 sq. km) with (1991 census) 94,385 inhabitants, containing the chief town, Mamoudzou (20,274 inhabitants); and the smaller island of Pamanzi (11 sq. km) lying 2 km to the east (9,775 in 1985) containing the old capital of Dzaoudzi (8,268). The whole territory covers 373 sq. km (144 sq. miles). The projected population for 2000 is 157,000.

The spoken language is Shimaoré (akin to Comorian, an Arabized dialect of Swahili), but French remains the official and commercial language.

Climate

The dry and sunniest season is from May to Oct. The hot but rainy season is from Nov. to April.

Constitution and Government

The island is administered by a General Council of 17 members, directly elected for a 6-year term. The French government is represented by an appointed Prefect. Mayotte is represented by 1 deputy in the National Assembly and by 1 member in the Senate. There are 17 communes, including 2 on Pamanzi.

Recent Elections

At the General council elections on 23 March 1997 the Mouvement Populaire Mahorais won 8 seats, the Rassemblement Mahorais pour la République 5, the Parti Socialiste 1 and others 5.

Current Administration

Prefect: Philippe Boisadam.

Economy

Currency

Since Feb. 1976 the currency has been the French franc.

Banking and Finance

The Institut d'Emission d'Outre-mer and the Banque Française Commerciale both have branches in Dzaoudzi and Mamoudzou.

Energy and Natural Resources

Electricity

Production (1993), 9·64m. kWh.

Agriculture

The area under cultivation in 1998 was 14,400 ha. The chief cash crops (1997) were: ylang-ylang 14,300 kg, vanilla 4,417 kg, cocoa-nut 2,060 kg, cinnamon 27,533 kg. The main food crops (1997) were bananas (30,200 tonnes) and cassava (10,000 tonnes). Livestock (1997): Cattle, 17,000; goats, 25,000; sheep, 2,000.

Forestry

There are some 19,750 ha of forest, of which 1,150 is primary, 15,000 secondary and 3,600 badlands (uncultivable or eroded).

Fisheries

A lobster and shrimp industry has been created. Production (1997): 1,500 tonnes.

Industry

Labour

In 1994, 18·5% of the active population was engaged in public building and works. In 1997 the minimum monthly wage (SMIC) was 39·29 francs an hour (6,664 a month).

International Trade

Imports and Exports

In 1997 exports of ylang-ylang totalled FF5·5m.; vanilla FF763,023; cocoa-nut FF2,075; cinnamon FF201,319. Imports (1993–94) totalled FF573·6m.

Trade Fairs

There are trade fairs every 2 years.

Communications

Roads

In 1994 there were 93 km of main roads and 137 km of local roads; and 1,528 motor vehicles.

Civil Aviation

There is an airport at Dzaoudzi, with scheduled services in 1998 provided by Air Austral to the Comoros, Kenya, Madagascar, Réunion and Zimbabwe, by Air Madagascar to Madagascar and Air Mauritius to Mauritius.

Shipping

There are services provided by Tratringa and Ville de Sima to Anjouan (Comores), and by Frégate des Îles to Mohéli, Moroni (Comores) and Majunga (Madagascar).

Telecommunications

In 1995 there were 5,300 telephone main lines.

Social Institutions

Justice

There is a *tribunal de première instance* and a *tribunal supérieur d'appel.*

Religion

The population is 97% Sunni Moslem, with a small Christian (mainly Roman Catholic) minority.

Education

In 1994 there were 25,805 pupils in nursery and primary schools, and 6,190 pupils at 7 *collèges* and 1 *lycée* at secondary level. There were also 1,922 pupils enrolled in pre-professional classes and professional *lycées*. There is a teacher training college.

Health

There were 2 hospitals with 100 beds in 1994. In 1985 there were 9 doctors, 1 dentist, 1 pharmacist, 2 midwives and 51 nursing personnel.

Culture

Broadcasting

Broadcasting is conducted by *Radio-Télévision Française d'Outre-Mer* (RFO-Mayotte) with 1 hour a day in Shimaoré. There are 2 private radio stations. In 1994 there were 30,000 radio and 3,500 TV receivers; colour is by SECAM.

Cinema

There is provision for 1 cinema, the Centre Mahoraise d'Animation Culturelle (CMAC), which operates either in Mamoudzou or Dzaoudzi.

Press

There was 1 weekly newspaper in 1997.

Tourism

In 1997 there were 8,545 visitors.

St Pierre and Miquelon

Key Historical Events
The only remaining fragment of the once-extensive French possessions in North America, the archipelago was settled from France in
the 17th century. It was a French colony from 1816 until 1976, an
overseas department until 1985, and is now a Territorial Collectivity.

Territory and Population
The archipelago consists of 2 islands off the south coast of
Newfoundland, with a total area of 242 sq. km, comprising the Saint-
Pierre group (26 sq. km) and the Miquelon-Langlade group (216 sq.
km). The population (1990 census) was 6,392, of whom 5,683 were
on Saint-Pierre and 709 on Miquelon. The projected population for
2000 is 7,000. The chief town is St Pierre.

The official language is French.

Social Statistics
1997: Births, 92; marriages, 36; divorces, 9; deaths, 51.

Constitution and Government
The Territorial Collectivity is administered by a General Council of 19
members directly elected for a 6-year term. It is represented in the
National Assembly in Paris by 1 deputy, in the Senate by 1 senator
and in the Economic and Social Council by 1 councillor. The French
government is represented by a Prefect.

Recent Elections
At the General Council elections on 20 March 1994, 12 seats went to
Archipel Demain, 3 to Objectifs Miquelonnais, 3 to Saint Pierre et
Miquelon 2000 and 1 to Miquelon Avenir.

Current Administration

Prefect: Rémi Thuau.
President of the General Council: Bernard Le Soavec.

Local Government

There are 2 municipal councils.

Economy

Budget

The budget for 1997 balanced at 245m. francs.

Currency

The French franc is in use. The Euro will be used as in metropolitan France.

Banking and Finance

Banks include the Banque des Îles Saint-Pierre et Miquelon, the Crédit Saint-Pierrais and the Caisse d'Épargne.

A Development Agency was created in 1996 to help with investment projects.

Energy and Natural Resources

Electricity

Production (1997): 43m. kWh.; installed capacity, 1995, 23 MW.

Agriculture

The islands, being mostly barren rock, are unsuited for agriculture, but some vegetables are grown and livestock is kept for local consumption.

Fisheries

In June 1992 an international tribunal awarded France a 24-mile fishery and economic zone around the islands and a 10·5-mile-wide corridor extending for 200 miles to the high seas. A Franco-Canadian agreement regulating fishing in the area was signed in Dec. 1994. Catch (1997): 89 tonnes, chiefly cod, lumpfish, snow-crab and shark. In 1986 the total catch had been more than 23,000 tonnes.

Industry

In 1994 there were 351 businesses (including 144 services, 69 public works, 45 food trade, 8 manufacturing and 2 agriculture). The main industry, fish processing, resumed in 1994 after a temporary cessation due to lack of supplies in 1992. Aquaculture is also of importance.

Labour

The economically active population in 1997 was 3,000. In 1997 the minimum wage (SMIC) was 39·29 francs per hour (6,664 a month). In 1996, 11% of the labour force was registered as unemployed.

International Trade

Imports and Exports

	1992	1993	1994	1995	1996
Imports	404	344	413	351	363
Exports	199	28	82	55	20

In 1996, 53% of imports came from Canada and 36% from France.

Communications

Roads

In 1996 there were 117 km of roads, of which 80 km were surfaced. There were 2,508 passenger cars and 1,254 commercial vehicles in 1996.

Civil Aviation

Canadian Airlines International connects St Pierre with Montreal, Halifax, Sydney (Nova Scotia) and St John's (Newfoundland). In

addition a new airport capable of receiving medium-haul aeroplanes
was due to open in 1999.

Shipping
St Pierre has regular services to Fortune and Halifax in Canada.
In 1996, 878 vessels called at St Pierre; 20,195 tonnes of freight were
unloaded and 1,873 tonnes were loaded.

Telecommunications
There were 4,165 telephones in 1996.

Social Institutions
Justice
There is a court of first instance and a higher court of appeal at
St Pierre.

Religion
The population is chiefly Roman Catholic.

Education
Primary instruction is free. There were, in 1995, 3 nursery and
5 primary schools with 793 pupils; 3 secondary schools with
549 pupils; and 2 technical schools with 152 pupils.

Health
There were (1995) 1 hospital with 44 beds, 1 convalescent home with
20, 1 retirement home with 40; 17 doctors and 1 dentist.

Culture
Broadcasting
Radio Télévision Française d'Outre-Mer (RFO) broadcasts in French
on medium-wave, and on 2 television channels (1 satellite). In 1997
there were 34 cable TV channels from Canada and the USA; and a
private local radio station (*Radio Atlantique*). In 1996 there were
about 4,850 radio and 3,350 TV sets in use.

Tourism

There were (1995) 13,760 foreign visitors, including 3,700 cruise visitors.

FURTHER READING

De La Rüe, E. A., *Saint-Pierre et Miquelon.* Paris, 1963

Ribault, J. Y., *Histoire de Saint-Pierre et Miquelon: des Origines à 1814.* St Pierre, 1962

Overseas Territories

Southern and Antarctic Territories

The Territory of the TAAF was created on 6 Aug. 1955. It comprises the Kerguelen and Crozet archipelagoes, the islands of Saint Paul and Amsterdam (formerly Nouvelle Amsterdam), all in the southern Indian ocean, and Terre Adélie. Since 2 April 1997 the administration has had its seat in Saint-Pierre, Réunion; before that it was in Paris. The Administrator is assisted by a 7-member consultative council which meets twice yearly in Paris; its members are nominated by the Government for 5 years. The 15-member Polar Environment Committee, which in 1993 replaced the former Consultative Committee on the Environment (est. 1982), meets at least once a year to discuss all problems relating to the preservation of the environment.

The French Institute for Polar Research and Technology was set up to organize scientific research and expeditions in Jan. 1992. The staff of the permanent scientific stations of the TAAF (120 in 1998) is renewed every 6 or 12 months and forms the only population.

Administrateur Supérieur: Mme Brigitte Girardin.

Kerguelen Islands

Situated 48–50° S. lat., 68–70° E. long.; consists of 1 large and 85 smaller islands, and over 200 islets and rocks, with a total area of

7,215 sq. km (2,786 sq. miles) of which Grande Terre occupies 6,675 sq. km (2,577 sq. miles). It was discovered in 1772 by Yves de Kerguelen, but was effectively occupied by France only in 1949. Port-aux-Français has several scientific research stations (56 members). Reindeer, trout and sheep have been acclimatized.

Crozet Islands

Situated 46° S. lat., 50–52° E. long.; consists of 5 larger and 15 tiny islands, with a total area of 505 sq. km (195 sq. miles). The western group includes Apostles, Pigs and Penguins islands; the eastern group, Possession and Eastern islands. The archipelago was discovered in 1772 by Marion Dufresne, whose mate, Crozet, annexed it for Louis XV. A meteorological and scientific station (17 members) at Base Alfred-Faure on Possession Island was built in 1964.

Amsterdam and Saint-Paul Islands

Situated 38–39° S. lat., 77° E. long. Amsterdam, with an area of 54 sq. km (21 sq. miles) was discovered in 1522 by Magellan's companions; Saint-Paul, lying about 100 km to the south, with an area of 7 sq. km (2·7 sq. miles), was probably discovered in 1559 by Portuguese sailors. Both were first visited in 1633 by the Dutch explorer, Van Diemen, and were annexed by France in 1843. They are both extinct volcanoes. The only inhabitants are at Base Martin de Vivies (est. 1949 on Amsterdam Island), including several scientific research stations, a hospital, communication and other facilities (20 members). Crayfish are caught commercially on Amsterdam.

Terre Adélie

Comprises that section of the Antarctic continent between 136° and 142° E. long., south of 60° S. lat. The ice-covered plateau has an area of about 432,000 sq. km (166,800 sq. miles), and was discovered in 1840 by Dumont d'Urville. A research station (27 members) is situated at Base Dumont d'Urville, which is maintained by the French Institute for Polar Research and Technology.

New Caledonia

Key Historical Events

New Caledonia was discovered by James Cook on 4 Sept. 1774. The first settlers (English Protestants and French Catholics) came in 1840. New Caledonia was annexed by France in 1853 and, together with most of its former dependencies, became an Overseas Territory in 1958.

Territory and Population

The territory comprises the island of New Caledonia and various outlying islands, all situated in the south-west Pacific with a total land area of 18,576 sq. km (7,172 sq. miles). The population (1996 census) was 196,836, including 67,151 Europeans (majority French), 86,788 Melanesians (Kanaks), 7,825 Vietnamese and Indonesians, 5,171 Polynesians, 17,763 Wallisians, 15,715 others. Density, 10 per sq. km. Projected population (2000): 200,000. The capital, Nouméa, had 76,293 inhabitants in 1996.

There are 4 main islands (or groups of):

New Caledonia

An area of 16,372 sq. km (about 400 km long, 50 km wide) with a population (1996 census) of 173,365. The east coast is predominantly Melanesian; the Nouméa region predominantly European; and the rest of the west coast is of mixed population.

Loyalty Islands

100 km (60 miles) east of New Caledonia, consisting of 3 large islands: Maré, Lifou and Uvéa, and many small islands. It has a total area of 1,981 sq. km and a population of 20,877, nearly all Melanesians, except on Uvéa which is partly Polynesian. The chief culture in the islands is coconuts; the chief export is copra.

Isle of Pines

A tourist and fishing centre 50 km (30 miles) to the south-east of Nouméa, with an area of 152 sq. km and a population of 1,671.

Bélep Archipelago

About 50 km north-west of New Caledonia, with an area of 70 sq. km and a population of 923.

The remaining islands are very small and have no permanent inhabitants. The largest are the Chesterfield Islands, a group of 11 well-wooded coral islets with a combined area of 10 sq. km, about 550 km west of the Bélep Archipelago. The Huon Islands, a group of 4 barren coral islets with a combined area of just 65 ha, are 225 km north of the Bélep Archipelago. Walpole, a limestone coral island of 1 sq. km, lies 150 km east of the Isle of Pines; Matthew Island (20 ha) and Hunter Island (2 sq. km), respectively 250 km and 330 km east of Walpole, are spasmodically active volcanic islands; and are also claimed by Vanuatu.

At the 1996 census there were 341 tribes (which have legal status under a high chief) living in 160 reserves, covering a surface area of 392,550 ha (21% of total land), and representing about 28·7 % of the population. 80,443 Melanesians belong to a tribe.

In addition to French, New Caledonia has a remarkable diversity of Melanesian languages (29 vernacular), divided into 4 main groups (Northern, Central, Southern and Loyalty Islands). There were 53,556 speakers (1996). The 3 most spoken forms are Drehu (11,338), Nengone (6,377) and Paicî (5,498). A ministerial decision in 1991 introduced local languages into the baccalauréat system. In 1997-98, 6 Melanesian languages were taught in schools.

Social Statistics

1997: Live births, 4,490; marriages, 1,005; divorces, 179; deaths, 1,016. Growth rate, 17·3 (per 1,000 population). Life expectancy at birth, 1990–95, 69·7 years for males and 74·7 years for females. Infant mortality, 1990–95, 22 per 1,000 live births; fertility rate, 2·7 births per woman.

Climate

Nouméa, Jan. 26·8°C, July 21°C (average temp., 24·1°C; max., 35·8°C; min., 14·5°C). Annual rainfall 1,171 mm.

Constitution and Government

Following constitutional changes introduced by the French government in 1985 and 1988, the Territory is administered by a High Commissioner assisted by a 4-member Consultative Committee, consisting of the President of the Territorial Congress (as President) and the Presidents of the 3 Provincial Assemblies. The French government is represented by the appointed High Commissioner.

There is a 54-member Territorial Congress consisting of the complete membership of the 3 Provincial Assemblies.

New Caledonia is represented in the French National Assembly by 2 deputies, in the Senate by 1 senator, in the Economic and Social Council by 1 councillor. The Territory is divided into 3 provinces, Nord, Sud and Îles Loyauté, each under a directly elected Regional Council. They are sub-divided into 32 communes administered by locally elected councils and mayors.

In Sept. 1987 the electorate voted in favour of remaining a French possession. Agreement was reached in June 1988 between the French government and representatives of both the European and Melanesian communities on New Caledonia, and confirmed in Nov. 1988 by plebiscites in both France and New Caledonia, under which the territory has been divided into 3 autonomous provinces.

On 5 May 1998 the Nouméa accords on limited autonomy were signed between the French government, the Rally for Caledonia in the Republic and the Kanak Socialist Front for National Liberation.

Recent Elections

On 8 Nov. 1998 there was a referendum for the agreement of the
Nouméa accords. The electorate was 106,716; turn-out was 74·2%.
Nearly 71·9% of those who voted said 'Yes' to the question 'Do you
approve the agreement on New Caledonia, signed in Nouméa on May
5 1998?'. Voting was restricted to those people resident in New
Caledonia before 1998.

In elections to the Territorial Congress on 9 May 1999, the conservative Rally for Caledonia in the Republic won 24 seats and the
National Liberation Front of the Socialist Kanaks 18, with other parties
and independents winning 4 seats or fewer.

Current Administration

High Commissioner: Dominique Bur.
President of the Territorial Congress: Simon Loueckhote (RPCR).

Economy

Performance

In 1996, the GDP was 335,482m. francs CFP; GDP per capita was
1·7m francs CFP.

Budget

The territorial budget for 1998 balanced at 71,800m. francs CFP.

Currency

The unit of currency is the franc CFP (XPF), with a parity of 18·18
to the French franc. 166,610m. francs CFP were in circulation in
Dec. 1996.

Banking and Finance

The banks are: Banque Calédonienne d'Investissement (BCI), the
Westpac Banking Corporation (WBC), the Banque Nationale de
Paris/Nouvelle-Calédonie (BNP/NC), the Société Générale

Calédonienne de Banque (SGCB), the Bank of Hawaii-Nouvelle-Calédonie (BoH-NC) and the Caisse d'Epargne.

Energy and Natural Resources
Electricity
Production (1997): 1,524,000 kWh.

Minerals
The mineral resources are extensive: nickel, chrome and iron abound; silver, gold, cobalt, lead, manganese, iron and copper have been mined at different times. The nickel deposits are of special value, being without arsenic, and constitute around 25% of the world's total nickel reserves. Production (1996, in 1,000 tonnes) of nickel ore, 7,266; the furnaces produced 11,239 tonnes of matte nickel and 42,173 tonnes of ferro-nickel.

Agriculture
According to the 1996 Census, 4,663 persons worked in the agricultural sector. The chief products are beef, pork, poultry, coffee, copra, maize, fruit and vegetables. Production (1996, in tonnes): Cereals, 1,730; coffee, 37; copra, 345; potatoes, 2,165; squash, 1,508.

Livestock (1996): cattle, 113,000; pigs, 39,000; goats (1995), 17,000; poultry (1995), 1m.

Forestry
There were 698,000 ha of forest in 1995, or 38·2% of the total land area (down from 38·3% in 1990). Timber production (1996), 1,244 tonnes.

Fisheries
In 1995 there were 302 fishing boats (1,768 GRT). Catch (1995): 5,292 tonnes. Aquaculture accounts for 25% (964·4 tonnes) of the world prawn market.

Industry

Local industries include chlorine and oxygen plants, cement, barbed wire, nails, pleasure and fishing boats, clothing, pasta, household cleaners, beer and soft drinks, confectionery and biscuits. The principal resource industries are nickel, fishing and tourism.

Labour

The working population (1996) was 64,377. The guaranteed monthly minimum wage was 76,207 francs CFP in Dec. 1997. In 1996 there were 30 industrial disputes and 13,826 working days were lost. There were 15,018 registered unemployed in 1997 (66% under 30 years of age).

International Trade

Imports and Exports

In 1996 the balance of trade showed a deficit of 42,863m. francs CFP. Imports and exports in 1m. francs CFP:

	1994	1995	1996	1997
Imports	87,305	86,896	93,088	97,700
Exports	41,706	51,235	50,225	55,912

In 1997, 41·9% of imports came from France, 13·3% from Australia; and 28·2% of exports went to France. Refined minerals (mainly ferro-nickel and nickel) accounted for 52% of exports; nickel ore, 26·8%; mattes, 13·1%.

Communications

Roads

There were (1996) 5,764 km of road, and 70,000 vehicles. In 1996 there were 623 road accidents and 42 fatalities.

Civil Aviation

New Caledonia is connected by air routes with France (by Air France and AOM), Australia (Air Calédonie International, AOM and Qantas Airways), New Zealand (Air Calédonie International and Air New Zealand), Japan (Air France and JAL), Sri Lanka (AOM), Guam (Continental Airlines), the Solomon Islands (Air Calédonie International and Solomon Airlines), the Fiji Islands (Air Calédonie International and Air Pacific), Vanuatu (Air Calédonie International and Air Vanuatu) and Wallis and Futuna (Air Calédonie International). Internal services with Air Calédonie link Nouméa to a number of domestic airfields. In 1996, there were 3,197 international movements via La Tontouta international airport, near Nouméa, carrying 311,538 passengers and 4,462 tonnes of freight.

Shipping

552 vessels entered Nouméa in 1996, unloading 1,091,400 tonnes of cargo and loading 4,950,700 tonnes.

Telecommunications

In 1997 there were 475,500 telephone main lines, and in 1995, 800 cellular phone subscribers and 2,200 fax machines.

Postal Services

In 1996 there were 42 post offices.

Social Institutions

Justice

There are courts at Nouméa, Koné and Wé (on Lifou Island), a court of appeal, a labour court and a joint commerce tribunal. There were 3,413 cases judged in the magistrates courts in 1996; 207 went before the court of appeal, 41 were sentenced in the court of assizes.

Religion

There were about 0·1m. Roman Catholics in 1994.

Education

In 1996 there were 36,139 pupils and 1,622 teachers in 279 primary schools; 26,276 pupils and 2,201 teachers in 69 secondary schools; and 1,749 students at university with 79 teaching staff; a further 68 were engaged in private further education. The state-funded French University of the Pacific (UFP) was founded in 1987 and comprises 2 campuses: 1 in New Caledonia (1,059 students in 1996); the other in French Polynesia. The South Pacific University Institute for Teacher Training, part of UFP, is based in Nouméa; there are 2 other colleges, in French Polynesia and Wallis and Futuna.

Health

In 1996 there were 362 doctors, 107 dentists, 74 pharmacists, 61 midwives and 1,208 paramedical personnel; there were 26 socio-medical districts, with 4 hospitals, 3 private clinics and 1,173 beds.

Welfare

There are 3 forms of social security cover: Free Medical Aid provides total sickness cover for non-waged persons and low-income earners; the Family Benefit, Workplace Injury and Contingency Fund for Workers (CAFAT); and numerous mutual benefit societies. In 1996 Free Medical Aid paid 53,055 beneficiaries a total of 8,298m. francs CFP; CAFAT paid 147,782 beneficiaries 12,874m. francs CFP in sickness cover.

Culture

Broadcasting

Radio Télévision Française d'Outre-Mer broadcasts in French on medium- and short-wave radio, and on 2 television channels; colour is by SECAM. There are also 3 commercial radio stations and 1 commercial TV channel (*Canal Plus*). There were 40,000 TV sets in 1996 and 102,000 radio receivers in 1995.

Cinema

In 1996, in Greater Nouméa, there were 11 cinemas and 1 drive-in.

Press

In 1998 there was 1 daily newspaper.

Tourism

Visitors (1996), 91,121 (30% French, 29% Japanese, 15·8% Australian). Receipts totalled US$109m. There were (1996) 76 hotels providing 2,075 beds.

FURTHER READING

Institut Territorial de la Statistique et des Etudes Économiques: *Journal Officiel de la Nouvelle Calédonie; Tableaux de l'Économie Calédonienne/New Caledonia: Facts & Figures (TEC 97)* (every 3 years*); Informations Statistiques Rapides de Nouvelle-Calédonie* (monthly).

Dommel, D., *La Crise Calédonienne: Démission ou Guérison?* Paris, 1993

Local statistical office: Institut Territorial de la Statistique et des Études Économiques, BP 823, 98845 Nouméa.

French Polynesia

Key Historical Events

French protectorates since 1843, these islands were annexed to France 1880–82 to form 'French Settlements in Oceania', which opted in Nov. 1958 for the status of an overseas territory within the French Community.

Territory and Population

The total land area of these 5 archipelagoes comprising 130 volcanic islands and coral atolls (76 inhabited) scattered over a wide area in the eastern Pacific, is 4,167 sq. km. The population (1996 census) was 219,521 (105,587 females); density, 53 per sq. km. At Dec.1998

French forces stationed in Polynesia numbered 2,119 (based mostly on Tahiti and the Hao atoll) and employed 1,162 Polynesian citizens. In 1995 an estimated 56·4% of the population lived in urban areas. Projected population (2025), 300,000.

The official languages are French and Tahitian.

The islands are administratively divided into 5 *circonscriptions* as follows:

Windward Islands
(Îles du Vent) (162,398 inhabitants, 1996) comprise Tahiti with an area of 1,042 sq. km and 150,707 inhabitants; Moeréa with an area of 132 sq. km and 11,682 inhabitants; Maiao (Tubuai Manu) with an area of 9 sq. km; and the smaller Mehetia and Tetiaroa. The capital is Papeete, Tahiti (79,024 inhabitants, including suburbs).

Leeward Islands
(Îles sous le Vent) comprise the 5 volcanic islands of Raiatéa, Tahaa, Huahine, Bora-Bora and Maupiti, together with 4 small atolls (Tupai, Mopelia, Scilly, Bellinghausen), the group having a total land area of 404 sq. km and 26,838 inhabitants in 1996. The chief town is Uturoa on Raiatéa. The Windward and Leeward Islands together are called the Society Archipelago (Archipel de la Société). Tahitian, a Polynesian language, is spoken throughout the archipelago and used as a *lingua franca* in the rest of the territory.

Marquesas Islands
12 islands lying north of the Tuamotu Archipelago, with a total area of 1,049 sq. km and 8,064 inhabitants in 1996. There are 6 inhabited islands: Nuku Hiva, Ua Pou, Ua Uka, Hiva Oa, Tahuata, Fatu Hiva; and 6 smaller (uninhabited) ones; the chief centre is Taiohae on Nukuhiva.

Austral or Tubuai Islands
lying south of the Society Archipelago, comprise a 1,300 km chain of volcanic islands and reefs. There are 5 inhabited islands (Rimatara,

Rurutu, Tubuai, Raivavae and, 500 km to the south, Rapa), with a combined area of 148 sq. km (6,563 inhabitants in 1996); the chief centre is Mataura on Tubuai.

Tuamotu Archipelago

consists of 2 parallel ranges of 76 atolls (53 inhabited) lying north and east of the Society Archipelago, and has a total area of 690 sq. km, with 15,370 inhabitants in 1996. The most populous atolls are Rangiroa (1,913 inhabitants), Hao (1,356) and Manihi (769).

The Mururoa and Fangataufa atolls in the south-east of the group were ceded to France in 1964 by the Territorial Assembly, and were used by France for nuclear tests from 1966-96. The cessation of nuclear testing marked the end of activities of the Pacific Testing Centre (CEP) in French Polynesia. The CEP was entirely dismantled during 1998. A small military presence remains to ensure permanent radiological control.

The *circonscription* also includes the Gambier Islands further east, with an area of 36 sq. km; the chief centre is Rikitea on the group's only inhabited island, Mangareva.

The uninhabited **Clipperton Island**, 1,000 km off the west coast of Mexico, is a dependency and is administered by the High Commissioner for French Polynesia but does not form part of the Territory; it is an atoll with an area of 5 sq. km.

Social Statistics

Annual population growth rate, 2·2%. Birth rate (1996) was 22·1 per 1,000 inhabitants; death rate, 4·7; marriage rate, 5·5; growth rate, 17·4. Life expectancy at birth, 1990–95, 68·3 years for males and 73·8 years for females. Infant mortality, 1990–95, 11 per 1,000 live births; fertility rate, 3·1 births per woman.

Climate

Papeete. Jan. 81°F (27·1°C), July 75°F (24°C). Annual rainfall 83" (2,106 mm).

Constitution and Government

Under the 1984 Constitution, the Territory is administered by a Council of Ministers, whose President is elected by the Territorial Assembly from among its own members; the President appoints a Vice-President and 14 other ministers (16 ministers in total in 1999). There is an advisory Economic and Social Committee. French Polynesia is represented in the French Assembly by 2 deputies, in the Senate by 1 senator, in the Economic and Social Council by 1 councillor. The French government is represented by a High Commissioner. The Territorial Assembly comprises 41 members elected every 5 years from 5 constituencies by universal suffrage, using the same proportional representation system as in metropolitan French regional elections. To be elected a party must gain at least 5% of votes cast. The Assembly elects a head of local government.

A statute drafted at the end of 1995 proposes to create French Polynesia as an Autonomous Overseas Territory in which the President of the Council of Ministers will become the President of the territory.

Recent Elections

Elections were held on 12 May 1996. The electorate was 125,000. 412 candidates stood. Rassemblement pour le Peuple (RPP; affiliated to the French Rassemblement pour la République) won 18 seats with 31·41% of votes cast; Polynesian Union, 14 with 23·27%; New Fatherland (NF), 5 with 12·28%; Independent Liberation Front of Polynesia, 4 with 11·43%. An RPR-NF coalition was subsequently formed under Gaston Flosse (RPR).

Current Administration

High Commissioner: Jean Aribaud.
President of the Council of Ministers: Gaston Flosse (RPR).

Economy

In decline since 1993, it has shown signs of recovery since 1997.

Performance

In 1997 GDP was FF21,600m. (5·5% up on 1996); GDP per capita
was FF96,964.

Budget

Total expenditure (1997), FF10,416m., of which FF6,744m. comes
directly from France.

Currency

The unit of currency is the franc CFP (XPF). Up to 31 Dec. 1998, its
parity was to the French franc: 1F CFP = 0·055 FF; from 1 Jan. 1999
parity was linked to the euro: 1,000 F CFP = 8·38 euros. Since 1 April
1967 currency issue in the three territories (New Caledonia, Wallis
and Futuna, French Polynesia) has been the responsibility of the
Institut d'Emission d'Outre-Mer (IEOM).

Banking and Finance

There are 4 commercial banks: Banque de Tahiti, Banque de
Polynésie, Société de Crédit et de Développement de l'Océanie,
and the Banque Westpac. There are also 22 credit institutions,
including SOFOTOM and the Agence Française de Développement
(AFD).

Energy and Natural Resources

French Polynesia is heavily dependent on external sources for its
energy. Since the early 1980s efforts have been made to reduce
this, which have included the development of solar energy. By 1999

it was estimated that production of solar energy was in the region of 2,700 hours a year.

Electricity
Production (1997) was 353m. kWh in 1994, of which 35% was hydro-electric. Consumption per capita (1995) was estimated to be 1,409 kWh. Between 1988 and 1997, 14,212 solar photovoltaic modules were installed in Polynesia.

Oil and Gas
In 1997 over 236,000 tonnes of combustible products were imported (with a value of FF346m.), mainly from Australia and Hawai; 8,600 tonnes of gas was imported.

Agriculture
Agriculture used to be the primary economic sector but now accounts for only a modest 8% (1997) of GDP. An important product is copra (coconut trees cover the coastal plains of the mountainous islands and the greater part of the low-lying islands); production (1997) 9,857 tonnes. A new and increasingly successful crop is the nono fruit, which has medicinal value. Exports of the nono reached FF15m. in 1998. Tropical fruits, such as bananas, pineapples and oranges, are grown for local consumption.

Livestock (1996): Cattle 7,000; pigs 42,000; goats (1995) 27,286; poultry (1995) 297,700.

Forestry
In 1999 there was between 4,000 and 5,000 ha of forest, 2,000 of it exploitable. The industry remains embryonic.

Fisheries
Polynesia has an exclusive zone of 5·2m. sq km, one of the largest in the world. The industry employs some 2,000 people, including 700 traditional fishermen. Catch (1997): 5,600 tonnes, almost exclusively

from sea fishing. Subject to annual agreement, a Korean fleet of 70 ships operates in the Polynesian waters; it had a quota of 3,000 tonnes in 1998–99.

Industry
Some 2,218 industrial enterprises employ 5,800 people. Principal industries include food and drink products, cosmetics, clothing and jewellery, furniture-making, metalwork and shipbuilding. Commerce is an important sector of the economy, employing (1997) some 7,400 persons in 2,448 enterprises across 1,752 retail and 696 manufacturing businesses.

International Trade
Imports and Exports
The trade balance is precarious: Polynesia imports a great deal and exports very little. The trade deficit in 1997 was FF4·15m. Total imports (1997), FF5·46m.; total exports, FF1·31m.

The chief exports are coconut oil, fish, nono juice, mother of pearl and cultured pearls. Pearl production in recent years has doubled, with FF794m. worth of pearls exported in 1998. Representing 27% of the world market, Polynesia is the world's second largest producer of pearls after Australia. It is the second largest industry in Polynesia after tourism, and employs some 4,000 islanders.

Major trading partners: France, Japan (66% of pearl exports), Hong Kong, the USA and the EU, with France accounting for over 38% of total imports and around 25% of exports in 1997, and the EU as a whole 52% of imports.

Communications
Roads
There were estimated to be 2,590 km of roads in 1999, 67% bitumenized.

Civil Aviation

The main airport is at Papeete (Tahiti-Faa'a). Air France and 8 other international airlines connect Tahiti International Airport with Paris, Auckland, Honolulu, Los Angeles, Santiago, Sydney, Tokyo and many Pacific islands. In 1998 Papeete handled 528,675 passengers (25% with Air France; 19% Air New Zealand; 17% AOM French Airlines). Local companies connect the islands with services from some secondary airports, including those at Bora-Bora, Rangiroa and Raiatea. Internal traffic handled 588,726 passengers and 2,200 tonnes of freight in 1997. Air Tahiti accounted for two-thirds of this; a further 6 local companies provide services from 48 secondary airfields.

Shipping

10 shipping companies connect France, San Francisco, New Zealand, Japan, Australia, South East Asia and most Pacific locations with Papeete. In 1997 727,000 tonnes of cargo were unloaded and 28,000 tonnes loaded at Papeete's main port. Around 1·4m. people pass through the port each year.

Telecommunications

Number of telephone main lines (1997), 52,300; mobile phones (1998), 11,000. In 1995 there were 900 fax machines.

Postal Services

There are (1999) 56 post offices, handling some 700 tonnes of post a year.

Social Institutions

Justice

There is a *tribunal de première instance* and a *cour d'appel* at Papeete.

Religion

In 1997 there were approximately 110,000 protestants (about 50% of the population) and 55,000 Roman Catholics (25%).

Education

There were (1998–99) 77,300 pupils and 5,200 teachers in 316 schools (46,800 in 255 primary schools; 30,500 in secondary school). The French University of the Pacific (UFP), founded in 1987, has 2 campuses, one in French Polynesia in Tahiti (the other in New Caledonia). The South Pacific University Institute for Teacher Training, founded in 1992 (part of UFP), has 3 colleges: in French Polynesia, Wallis and Futuna, and in Nouméa (New Caledonia), where it is headquartered. In 1997–98, 2,200 students followed university courses.

Health

There were (1999) 1 territorial hospital centre, 4 general hospitals, 1 specialist hospital and 2 private clinics, with a total of 855 beds. Medical personnel numbered 1,590 persons, including 384 doctors (175 per 100,000 inhabitants), 94 dentists and 51 pharmacists. Health spending accounted for 10·2% of GDP in 1997.

Welfare

In 1997, 202,760 people benefitted from social welfare.

Culture

Broadcasting

There are 3 TV broadcasters (1 public, 2 independent): *Radio Télévision Française d'Outre-mer* (RFO) which broadcasts on 2 channels in French, Tahitian and English; *Canal + Polynésie*; and *Telefenua* which broadcasts across 16 channels. There are also 11 private radio stations. Number of receivers (1999): radio, 40,350; TV, 40,000.

Cinema

There are 4 cinemas in Papeete.

Press

In 1999 there were 2 daily newspapers.

Tourism

Tourism is the main industry. There were 189,000 tourist arrivals in 1998. Total revenue (1997) FF2m.

FURTHER READING

Bounds, J. H., *Tahiti*. Bend, Oregon, 1978

Luke, Sir Harry, *The Islands of the South Pacific*. London, 1961

O'Reilly, P. and Reitman, E., *Bibliographie de Tahiti et de la Polynésie française*. Paris, 1967

O'Reilly, P. and Teissier, R., *Tahitiens. Répertoire bio-bibliographique de la Polynésie française*. Paris, 1963

Local statistical office: Institut Territorial de la Statistique, Papeete.

Wallis and Futuna

Key Historical Events

French dependencies since 1842, the inhabitants of these islands voted on 22 Dec. 1959 by 4,307 votes out of 4,576 in favour of exchanging their status to that of an overseas territory, which took effect from 29 July 1961.

Territory and Population

The territory comprises two groups of islands in the central Pacific (total area 240 sq. km, over 14,000 inhabitants in 1996). The projected population for 2000 is 15,000. The Îles de Hoorn lie 255 km north-east of the Fiji Islands and consist of 2 main islands: Futuna (64 sq. km, 5,000 inhabitants) and uninhabited Alofi (51 sq. km).

The Wallis Archipelago lies another 160 km further north-east, and has an area of 159 sq. km (9,000 inhabitants). It comprises the main island of Uvéa (60 sq. km; over 1,000 inhabitants) on Uvéa. Wallisian and Futunian are distinct Polynesian languages.

Social Statistics

Estimates per 1,000 population, 1998: birth rate, 23·0; death rate, 4·8.

Constitution and Government

A Prefect represents the French government and carries out the duties of head of the territory, assisted by a 20-member Territorial Assembly directly elected for a 5-year term, and a 6-member Territorial Council, comprising the 3 traditional chiefs and 3 nominees of the Prefect agreed by the Territorial Assembly. The territory is represented by 1 deputy in the French National Assembly, by 1 senator in the Senate, and by 1 member on the Economic and Social Council. There are 3 districts: Singave and Alo (both on Futuna), and Wallis; in each, tribal kings exercise customary powers assisted by ministers and district and village chiefs.

Recent Elections

Territorial Assembly elections were held in March 1992.
The electorate was 6,972; 5,657 votes were cast.

Current Administration

Chief Administrator: Christian Dors.
President of the Territorial Assembly: Victor Brial (RPR).

Economy

Budget
The budget for 1997 balanced at 120,100m. French francs.

Currency

The unit of currency is the franc CFP (XPF), with a parity of 18·18 to the French franc.

Banking and Finance

There is a branch of Indosuez at Mata-Utu.

Energy and Natural Resources

Electricity

There is a thermal power station at Mata-Utu.

Agriculture

The chief products are copra, cassava, yams, taro roots and bananas.

Livestock (1996): 25,000 pigs; 7,000 goats.

Fisheries

The catch in 1995 was 170 tonnes.

Communications

Roads

There are about 100 km of roads on Uvéa.

Civil Aviation

There is an airport on Wallis, at Hihifo, and another near Alo on Futuna. 5 flights a week link Wallis and Futuna. Air Calédonie International operates 2 flights a week to Nouméa and 1 a week to French Polynesia.

Shipping

A regular cargo service links Mata-Utu (Wallis) and Singave (Futuna) with Nouméa (New Caledonia).

Telecommunications

There were 340 telephones in 1985.

Postal Services

There were 6 post offices in 1986.

Social Institutions

Justice

There is a court of first instance, from which appeals can be made to the court of appeal in New Caledonia.

Religion

The majority of the population is Roman Catholic.

Education

In 1993 there were 3,624 pupils in primary schools and 1,777 in secondary schools. The South Pacific University Institute for Teacher Training, founded in 1992 (part of the French University of the Pacific, UFP) has 3 colleges: in Wallis and Futuna, French Polynesia and Nouméa (New Caledonia), where it is headquartered.

Health

In 1991 there was 1 hospital with 60 beds, and 4 dispensaries.

Culture

Broadcasting

There were 2 radio stations in 1986.